Life Beneath The Arch

Life Beneath The Arch

CHARLES ARCH

with Lyn Ebenezer

First impression: 2018

© Copyright Charles Arch and Y Lolfa Cyf., 2018

The contents of this book are subject to copyright, and may
not be reproduced by any means, mechanical or electronic,
without the prior, written consent of the publishers.

The author wishes to thank Professor David Austin
and Dr Terence Williams for the use of their photographs

The publishers wish to acknowledge the support of
Cyngor Llyfrau Cymru

Cover photograph: Iestyn Hughes,
with thanks to CADW for their cooperation
Cover design: Y Lolfa

ISBN: 978 1 78461 528 4

Published and printed in Wales
on paper from well-maintained forests by
Y Lolfa Cyf., Talybont, Ceredigion SY24 5HE
website www.ylolfa.com
e-mail ylolfa@ylolfa.com
tel 01970 832 304
fax 832 782

Foreword

IT IS A privilege to write a foreword to a book that discusses the influence of the monks of Strata Florida on the local community, and particularly on agriculture.

The furthest my family farming at Cwm-meurig can go is 'Morgan' in around 1625. This was before the advent of surnames. Since the community must have been fairly well settled and unlikely to have moved a great deal, they must have been beneficiaries of the wisdom and practices of the monks. It was a Morgan Jenkins who later first used horses rather than oxen to pull the plough. The Jenkinses were tenants at Cwm-meurig until they were evicted in 1875.

I am always amazed that it took Thomas Johnes of Hafod to introduce the use of dogs to round up sheep. This must have been equally as innovative.

Rt Hon. Lord Morris of Aberavon, KG, QC

Contents

Introduction

I HAVE REASON to thank a number of people for their contribution in making it possible to publish this book. Firstly, I have to acknowledge the part played by the people I was born among and lived in their midst for so long. Having left for a prolonged period, I am now back home again.

The influence of various relatives and friends has been immense, people such as Miss Rees, John Jenkins, Dafydd Hughes and Mary Roberts (Miss Boden), my ex-Welsh teacher at Tregaron. And was there ever a philosopher that could touch Dai Cornwal?

The original account in Welsh would not have appeared without the aid of my wife Mari's biro and my daughter Mererid's typewriter and the great diligence shown by Lyn Ebenezer in putting everything together in good order.

This is an extended translation of the original Welsh version and, like its predecessor, it is an attempt to record the history of a certain period in my life and to pay tribute to a neighbourhood and those individuals who made it a warm and welcoming community. They are people I will cherish and whose memory I will treasure all my life.

Finally, as one of the Arch family who was born and bred beneath the Great Arch of the Abbey, my thanks to the monks of Strata Florida who started it all.

Charles Arch

June 2018

1

The Great Escape

ALTHOUGH I WAS born in the shadow of the great western archway of Strata Florida Abbey – the iconic image that best personifies the twelfth-century Cistercian monastery – it is another gateway that still haunts my earliest memories. It was a chained garden gate that incarcerated me within the confines of our back yard. Completing my place of confinement were two other gates, on either end. Peering between the bars of that central gate I could only imagine what I was missing beyond my open prison. Between those bars I could see not only a substantial part of the farmyard but also the road that led to the mountains, and the brook beyond the pine end of the barn.

The two end gates were too heavy for me to open. My mother kept the middle gate locked in the interest of health and safety well before the phrase became the bastion and bane of daily life. I was, apparently, a wanderer by nature. From the day I started walking I would, according to my mother, aim for the back door. Should that be open, the garden gate opposite would be the only obstacle between me and the wash house and ultimately the stream beyond the yard.

I was the first-born. Naturally, no one wanted me to disappear. And so the three gates curtailed my wanderlust.

The ancient farmhouse was fringed with a surfaced road. Three sides of the building were edged with a substantial stone wall. The intervening space was further enclosed with the oblong garden gate and the two wooden gates at each end, allowing me the limited freedom of some twenty-five feet by eight feet. This should have offered ample space to any ordinary child, but not to one who yearned to wander around the farmyard and inevitably wet his feet in the brook while crossing it in order to see the wider world beyond.

Not that my open prison did not have its attractions. The water tap on the wall was particularly tempting. It was situated opposite the back door so that it would be convenient for the kitchen. I had watched Mam and Bet the maid draw water from it, and gradually I managed to master their secret. After a few soakings, however, Mam's admonitions taught me the error of my ways.

Occasionally one of our menagerie of farm cats would join me. There are two kinds of beings one should never trust: cats and politicians. It took some time before I realised the fickleness of the latter breed. But, as for the former, it took very little time. Often, one of these sly creatures would slink towards me pretending to be friendly. I would stroke its back, the creature's purring professing pleasure. Then, suddenly, it would unsheathe its claws and strike, leaving red furrows along the back of my hand.

One day I found some stale bread with which I managed to tempt Wag the black-and-white sheepdog to join me. Suddenly, a cockerel flew over the wall and started pecking away at some stray crumbs. This was a new game. I grabbed the unsuspecting bird by the tail. Then, all at once, the cockerel was gone, leaving me with a plume of tail feathers in my hand. The bird escaped minus tail and also minus its dignity.

Sometimes my incarceration would mean solitary confinement. This would often lead to a tantrum. No matter which gate I looked through, no one would be available to humour me. Through one gate I would, perhaps, see a parade of cows passing by dispassionately, nonchalantly chewing their cuds. Through another I would see my father or one of the farmhands hurrying past. Sometimes, someone would pass in or out through one of the gates, always remembering to close it securely behind them. Usually it would be Bet carrying two bucketfuls of gruel at a time for the calves. The gruel would be boiled in the big cauldron on the kitchen fire. I could hear it spluttering away. On such occasions the kitchen would be forbidden territory unless I was being safely escorted by Bet. Her iron grip on my hand meant that such adventures soon lost their appeal.

Occasionally Uncle John, leaning heavily on his walking stick, would join me. But no amount of pleading on my part would persuade him to open the garden gate. He was immune to my cajoling and soon he would abandon me to my boredom.

One day Bet was carrying two buckets of gruel to the calves when Mam called her from upstairs. Bet left the full buckets by the gate and went back in. At once Wag scrambled in over the gate and began scoffing gruel from one of the buckets. And that's when I realised that Wag had shown me a means of escape. I began climbing the gate and managed to get one leg over it. And there I was, stuck. I looked down and I could see the ground coming up to meet me. Luckily, Bet returned and rescued me. But I attempted my escape another three times over the coming days until I eventually saw the light. I realised that I should place both feet firmly on the highest bar but one of the gate, grab hold of the upper bar and lift one leg over and then the other and then drop down. And there I was, standing outside the gate. Freedom!

I looked around. Where to next, I wondered? There were so many choices. Everywhere I looked there were buildings. And there were doors to open. To the right was the wash house and the peat shed. Between them and me was the road, but I could cross that without any problem. The farmyard formed a square, the cowshed being one of the sides. The store cattle shed was on another. Then came the barn and the bull's shed. And completing the square were the stable and cart shed.

The farmyard gates would normally have been shut. But, even closed, they would not have presented much of a problem. There was only one awkward gate, the one that led to the end wall of the barn and to the rickyard. This was covered with a sheep mesh, meaning that there was a danger of my feet getting entangled in it should I attempt to climb the gate. And I knew that if I was trapped there, I wouldn't be able to cry for help without betraying my escape.

I soon realised that the farmyard was nowhere near as interesting as I had imagined it to be. For one thing, there were too many people around. Should I, for instance, try to follow my father around the place he would not allow me to do so. If I tried to follow him to the barn or the stable, he would grab me and I would be back in the house in no time. There, I had no one to follow around, save for Bet from bedroom to bedroom as she did the cleaning. How I hated those rooms that reeked of polish, especially the servants' quarters that also smelled of stale pee.

Occasionally I would escape detection long enough to visit the white cow in its stall. She was completely white save for a few black hairs around her mouth and ears. But, as soon as the cow and I began enjoying ourselves, we would be interrupted by the cowman, Jack Sais, who would mumble something in a language I didn't understand. And that would be the end of the fun.

Jack was short and tubby, and after years of wandering he had settled down in the area. His real name was John Kirk but he was known to all as Jack Sais, meaning English Jack. Like all the tramps who helped out, Jack loved eating. His appetite knew no bounds. One night, while eating his supper, he asked Mam for some vinegar. She invited him to help himself from the bottle in the corner cabinet. Jack poured a goodly amount over his food.

'Nice vinegar this, missus,' said Jack.

He shook more vinegar over his food. Mam then realised that it wasn't vinegar that Jack was pouring out so liberally. It was elderberry wine!

Jack died in September 1949 and he is buried at Strata Florida cemetery. There is a blue gravestone marking his last place of rest. It was paid for from a fund organised by Jack Jenkins who collected money from among the locals. I never saw Jack Sais without him wearing a pair of corduroy trousers and carrying either a yard brush or a pitchfork.

The stable was my favourite place, with its shire horses and my father's riding pony in the far stall. When Lester, the bay mare, kicked the cobbles, its horseshoes would create a shower of sparks. My ambition was to catch those sparks in a bucket. But every time I attempted to do so Uncle Jack or Tanto, one of the servants, would appear. And that would be the end of another game. Life was like that. Every time I began enjoying myself, a grown-up would come along and spoil everything. Grown-ups were useless people, devoid of any kind of imagination.

One morning, as I stood on the bluestone slab outside the stable door, I saw Tanto combing the mane of Darbi, the roan pony. He was sitting on the stall partition as he plaited ribbons in and out of the mane. Normally, upon seeing me, he would cuddle me. Not this time. He was too engrossed in his work. I was so disappointed with being ignored that I went into a strop. Tanto immediately tried to calm me down.

'Come on now, that's a good boy!' he comforted me.

He then picked me up and placed me on the pony's back. There I sat, my head almost touching the ceiling, with Tanto holding on to one of my legs just in case I slipped. For the first time in my life I was riding!

From that moment on Tanto became my friend. He was short and dark haired and as supple as a leather thong. According to Mam no one could touch him as a poacher. Often we would dine on rabbits or fish caught by Tanto. He then got married, had lots of children and became a lorry driver.

2

Beyond the Gate

OUR HOUSE WAS a strange place. It was always full of people yet I had no one to play with. They were all old, all save for my sister. She merely slept and cried in her pram all day. Sometimes I would pull on her hair, trying to raise her on her feet. Then, hearing her screeching, either Mam or Bet would rush over and send me out.

Sometimes I would escape to the pigsties where, by climbing one of the doors, I could scratch the black breeding sow's back. The black sow was one of my friends. As soon as I began scratching her back she would force herself closer to the door so that I could reach her with less effort. One morning I overheard Mam saying that the black sow had given birth to a litter of piglets.

'Ten black piglets, each one with a white strip along their backs,' she told Bet.

Off I sneaked to the sty where I rattled the latch to draw the sow's attention before climbing onto the door. But she wouldn't come out and I never saw her litter. After that I kept away. The place stank anyway.

Sometimes I would tempt Fly the sheepdog, with the lure of a sandwich or a piece of cake, to accompany me. Fly was short-legged, her body a mixture of black, white and red. One day Fly was helping herself to gruel left by Bet once again. After eating to her heart's content she then left past the wash house. Feeling a bit disappointed that she had decided not to linger with me, I decided to follow her. She crawled under Cae Bach gate and turned towards the hay shed. There, in a nest of dry hay, nestled eight pups yelping and whimpering impatiently. Fly lay down and immediately her newborn pups began suckling her. I spent hours fondling them all in turn. Then Jack Sais, carrying hay in a canvas sling, saw what was happening and tried to send me home. He couldn't see that Fly and I had an understanding.

The following morning when I returned, there was only one puppy left, a black one, and Fly was whining and looking for the others. I searched for the other seven everywhere but there was no sign of them anywhere. I questioned all the men who were around the place but they insisted that Fly had given birth to just the one puppy. I realised once more that grown-ups were strange people.

Another thing about grown-ups was that whenever I would ask one of them to play with me they would inevitably refuse. They always had something more important to do. Yet Tanto and Uncle Jack would spend hours sitting around smoking and chatting.

During the evenings, especially in winter, the house would be full of people. In the parlour would be Miss Davies, a teacher at the nearby school, and a man always referred to as Davies the Ruins. Davies' job was to oversee the clearing of soil and rubble from parts of the old abbey site next door. Both of them were lodgers and neither of them had Christian names. I would sometimes visit the parlour and Davies the Ruins would always be nice to me. Sometimes he would give me treats. Miss Davies was rather taciturn and she would usually ignore me.

I learnt later that Miss Davies was an unmarried woman and lived in Lampeter. She would return home every Friday evening either on the bus or by train from Strata Florida station. She would always be back by Monday morning. Davies the Ruins was from the north and would use some words that I couldn't understand. He also talked relatively quickly. Some of the men would refer to him as a 'bloody Gog', but he was rather nice. Mam told me he was from a place called Dolwyddelan, a real north Wales place. He would not go home very often, only about once every three weeks or a month as he had to travel far. There were tons of rubble to clear from the abbey grounds. He was keeping the place tidy for the visitors during the summer. He would always refer to the place as the 'Abbey'. But Tanto and Uncle Jack would always beg to differ.

'Abbey!' they would say. 'It's not the Abbey; it's the bloody Ruins!'

Whether it should be the Abbey or the Ruins, the site was ideal for us children as a playground. To our headmistress, Miss Rees, it was sacrilege to refer to the place as anything but 'Strata Florida Abbey'. And she would proudly add, 'burial place of Dafydd ap Gwilym and a host of princes'. It is said that the old farmhouse was once a part of the abbey itself. In the parlour there is still a most interesting artefact, a panel painting of Christ being tempted by the Devil. Some have argued that the unknown artist was a Cistercian monk, and no one has been able to prove what type of wood the panel consists of or even in what country the timber could have grown.

Embracing the abbey is the parish cemetery and church. The site is about a mile and a half from the village of Pontrhydfendigaid (Bont). Sometimes, after school, Dick John and his brother Charles from nearby Cornwal cottage would join me in playing games in the abbey grounds. We would spend hours playing hide-and-seek among the many nooks and crannies. One day, we thought we had discovered a dead body in a tunnel beneath one of the chapels. We went running to fetch my father only to discover that it was Harry Lauder, an old tramp sleeping and sobering up following one of his binges.

Looking back, it is probable that from among my senses the first that I became aware of was fear. Time and again after school I would be sent on errands to the village. Often, especially in winter, it would be dark. My father's advice was,

'If something frightens you, and if you feel there's something unnatural out there, stop still for a while and then continue.'

Easier said than done. The moon tends to play tricks on you. I was always apprehensive as I approached the cemetery gate. I once remember a particularly dark night on my way home from the village. Some fifty yards from the cemetery I saw four small white figures on the ground and a fifth hovering above them. I stood still. Not because I recalled my father's advice but because I was petrified. After a while I crept forwards slowly, my legs quaking. Then I realised that I was looking at my father's best shire horse, a black stallion with four white legs and a white stripe down its forehead. There were other occasions when I felt scared but remembering this particular incident always gave me the strength to carry on.

The abbey provided us country children with the opportunity over the years of meeting visitors, many from abroad. Over the Second World War years my mother was the custodian of the abbey and it was incredible, even in those dark and dangerous times, that the place attracted so many visitors. For some years now there has been a full-time custodian and the old place has been cleared of the mounds of waste earth and stone that littered it.

The rubble was dumped in a corner of one of our fields. The man who did all the heavy work was Tom Thomas who lived in Terrace Road. He would be at it all day, every day, shifting barrow loads of rubble. Should his digging reveal any artefacts such as a tile or a piece of pottery, they would be salvaged for examination by archaeologists. I would often watch Tom at work. He was a large man, rather morose but harmless. He always carried a watch in his breast pocket and I would always make a point of asking him the time so that I could hear his inevitable reply,

'Don't ask again, that's a good lad. The watch tends to wear out if I take it out too often.'

The best part of the day would be evening in the spacious kitchen, with the supper eaters occupying chairs around two tables, one large the other small. I would always try to sit in front of the larger table between Tanto and Uncle Jack. I hated sitting next to Jack Sais. His clothes always smelt of cow dung. He would eat like a horse and would belch all the time, sometimes in my face.

After we had eaten, the smaller table would be cleared and placed at the far end of the kitchen. Then Uncle Jack would fetch the quoits board and place it on the table. The square board consisted of two inner circles of different colours, and a metal peg jutted up from the centre. When the board wasn't being used, four rubber rings were kept on the peg. These large rings would be coloured black on one side and white on the other. Four of the men would form two pairs. The aim, of course, was to throw the rings at the peg and, if possible, encircle it or at least come as close as possible to doing so. I yearned to play every night but I was only allowed one conciliatory throw before the grown-ups took over. Fair play to Uncle John, before the game began in earnest he would say,

'Give the little one a shot.'

Sometimes his words fell on deaf ears and I would grab the rings and run away with them and hide under the big table. That would be the cue for Bet to appear and drag me out to be washed and sent to bed. Had I been given the chance to play, I would have been just as good as any of them. But only Uncle John appreciated that.

Uncle John was old, forever leaning on his walking stick. He always carried sweets in his pocket but he wouldn't share them with me unless I sat with him to talk. Sometimes I would be ready to sacrifice the sweets, especially when he broke wind. He was always chewing tobacco and spitting into the fire, a brown dribble staining his lips and chin.

Often when Tanto or Uncle Jack would see me on the yard they would grab a tuft of my hair and mock me.

'You look like a girl!' or 'Come here so I can cut your hair!'

Usually I would ignore them. Grown-ups were forever saying stupid things. But, one day, Mam and Father were away somewhere and Bet was upstairs tending to my little sister Beti. It was just after dinner and Beti was crying, probably from want of sleep. Suddenly, Tanto took from his pocket a bag of liquorish drops. We called them 'London Mice Droppings'. He offered me one on condition that I sat on the end of the table. I complied immediately. And there I sat munching liquorish drops and ignoring the fact that Uncle Jack was meddling with my hair. He was holding a pair of scissors. I could see bits of hair falling around me. But I carried on eating Tanto's sweets. For a change, both Tanto and Uncle Jack were in high spirits. Suddenly, Uncle Jack announced,

'There you are!'

I saw a shadow cross the doorway. Mam was back. When she saw what had happened she sat down and cried. As for Tanto and Uncle Jack, they crept out looking as sheepish as Fly did whenever she would be caught in the dairy. Then Bet arrived from upstairs. She cried as well. Mam and Bet brushed up my sheared locks and put them in a box. I was totally unperturbed, polishing off the liquorish drops. I had always believed that only babies cried. Years later I discovered my light-coloured curls nestling in a fig box in a drawer in Mam's dresser. She had kept them over all the years. And then I cried.

After I had served my time in my open prison I would sometimes slip away quietly past the gable end of the stable and turn the corner of the garden towards the river. The river was a great place for adventures. I would wade in to a pool up to my knees and laugh at seeing the refraction of the light on the water making my legs look bandy. Often a tiddler would dart under a stone. But whenever I lifted the stone, there would be nothing there. Wet clothes were a nuisance and I had to remove them should I want to continue with my adventures. But the fun would always be short-lived. Bet would inevitably appear. She would drag me back to the house and I would have to spend the next hour or two having to follow her as she cleaned the bedrooms.

Shearing day was one of the main events on the farm calendar. Every farm had its set date. The first in the area would be Nantyrhwch on the last Monday in June. We would hold ours on the following Thursday. During the week leading up to that date there would be a hive of activity. Mam and Beti would be decorating. Jack Sais would whitewash the cowshed. The rest of the men would be harvesting green ferns to spread around as a cushion for the sheep. Another sure giveaway that shearing day was upon us was the arrival of neighbours on horseback. Our own horse, Billy Boy, would already be here of course. Billy had a chestnut coat with white fetlocks. He was a good trotter. The horses would cause a furore of neighing and the stamping of hooves as one of the horses attempted to mount a filly. Should Billy attempt this, Father would not be happy. I chided him, believing that it was unfair. But Father would always change the subject.

One day I had a brainwave. I asked Uncle John to cut me a strong sapling and find me a length of string. I made the string into a head halter and tied it to the stick. I then led the stick around the yard pretending I was leading Billy Boy.

Once I wandered further than usual along the riverbank so that I could be alone. Then, as I was about to wade into the water, I suddenly heard children's voices. But I couldn't see anyone around. Lower down, there was a building that I had never seen before. I had never been that far previously as Bet would have surely caught me and taken me home. I approached the small building. The door was open and inside the place was full of children. And pointing at a blackboard leaning on an upright easel was Miss Davies. I wandered in among a crowd of children playing with all kinds of toys on the floor. I had never seen so many toys. I stayed there for most of the day. I returned there day after day for some time afterwards. But, during all that time, not once did Bet come over to take me home.

3

Off to School

SCHOOL WAS A disappointment. It wasn't as exciting as I had been led to believe. At home I was free to run around, and if my pyjama trousers slipped down over my hips and became a hindrance I would simply discard them. Then I would start running again.

I would slip into the milk pantry where Bet would be turning the separator handle round and round. If I stretched my legs and stood on tiptoe, I would be able to peep into the dark brown earthenware bowl that held the cream. And if Bet wasn't looking I would stick a finger into the cream and lick the rich yellow liquid. My finger would leave its trace on the surface of the cream, but the falling yellow flow would soon obliterate the evidence, allowing me to escape and leave Bet none the wiser.

Occasionally Mam would forget to place the barrier across the kitchen door. This would allow me to slip quietly into the nook under the dresser where I would hide. Then, as soon as Mam turned her back, I would be off like a shot through the open door and into the front parlour where I would hide behind the hall stand that held walking sticks and umbrellas. From there I would be able to peer into the next room where Miss Davies and Davies the Ruins were eating their breakfast. They would always be deep in conversation, discussing things that I could never understand. I wondered how Miss Davies was allowed to teach children.

Mam would always jam the door of that room open using a chair so that she could carry food from the kitchen to feed Miss Davies and Davies the Ruins. This allowed me easy access. It also allowed me an escape route out to the rear of the house. Sometimes, as I stood there, Tanto or Jack Sais would trundle past carrying two buckets overflowing with milk from the cowshed, the froth billowing out over the rims. As they passed I would slyly grab a handful of froth and run off and hide behind the gable end of the wash house. There I would close both palms gently over the froth, leaving a little space between my fingers. I would then blow softly, and gradually a cloud of small white bubbles would emerge. They soon burst. But once, a single small bubble hovered over the roof of the shed and landed somewhere in the Back Field. After I had blown the froth bubbles, Fly would sidle over to lick my fingers clean. Sometimes she spoiled the fun by licking my fingers before I had even blown on them.

But schooldays brought an end to my fun. For one thing, I had to be washed twice a day. Evenings would see Mam or Bet, or even Father sometimes, dumping me in a large metal bath full of water in front of the fire. As if that wasn't enough, they would put something in the water and when I came out my bottom would be red and smarting. It was only much later that I came to realise what that hot yellow liquid was. It came in a small flat bottle and had letters written on it. They spelt D-E-T-T-O-L. Only a few drops were poured into the water but my bottom would burn for a good half-hour afterwards. Then, rather than being allowed to stay and enjoy the fun in the kitchen, I would hear the same old story,

'Come on now, or you will be too tired to go to school tomorrow.'

What a shabby trick, just to stop me playing a game of rings! They would then be able to carry on talking away to each other loudly. With me there they would only whisper to each other. But I wasn't interested in their silly talk. They could whisper to each other to their hearts' content if they wanted to. All I wanted was to play.

Miss Davies started acting very oddly after I started attending school. For a while she would leave ahead of me every morning and when I arrived she would give a wan little smile as if she didn't want anyone to see that she was smiling. And if William or Dick stole my modelling clay, she would hardly ever come to my aid and would never scold the other two for acting so shamefully. Many was the time I told Mam about this and I urged her not to provide Miss Davies with any breakfast as punishment for her lack of concern. But Mam would just smile and change the subject.

One day when I arrived home from school I saw Dr Davies talking to Father at the back door. The doctor carried a little black leather bag.

'Don't you go running around and make a racket upstairs tonight,' he said. 'Give your mam and the baby a chance to sleep.'

A baby! No one had bothered telling me before I left for school that morning. The doctor must have brought it in that strange little black bag he was carrying. But before I could ask, Bet arrived and held my hand.

'Come and see the new baby,' she said.

Bet led me upstairs and there, lying next to Mam in bed, was this small, wizened baby looking angry, its fists clenched and with a head shaped like a potato.

'Say hello to your new little sister,' said Mam.

The baby was Beti, of course. I immediately lost all interest. There we were living on a large farm and Mam and Father had decided to order a girl! I wanted a brother, someone I could play with and go to school together. And if Dick tried to steal my modelling clay again, then there would be two of us to deal with him. But no, Mam and Father had decided on a girl. It's hard to understand the minds of grown-ups sometimes.

Almost without my realising it, probably because I was spending so much time in school, my sister Beti was growing and had started walking and, indeed, she would sometimes even play with me. She was apt to cry if I pushed her or pulled her hair. But sometimes it would be fun. By the summer months, Beti and I would spend some time playing in the front garden while Mam and the new maid were milking. Bet had left during the winter for some unknown reason.

Glenys, another new baby, arrived. Mam must have realised I was growing up. Sometimes, when Glenys was left in her pram in the front garden, Mam would ask me to keep an eye on her and give a shout if the baby was crying. If Mam and the maid were milking and the men were out haymaking, Glenys' pram would be parked outside the cowshed door.

Things went well for a while; Beti and I playing and the baby asleep for most of the time. But, far too often, the baby would spite us by waking up and her screaming would interrupt our playing. One day, with Glenys screaming for longer than usual, I went over to the pram and started rocking it gently as Mam would often do. And, to my surprise, the screaming stopped. I could see from looking at Beti's face that she was impressed. But, as we resumed our playing, the screaming started again. This time Beti joined me and we both rocked the pram. However, with both of us involved, the pram turned over. The crying stopped but there was no sign of the baby! We searched through the blankets, but Glenys wasn't there. We were laughing, but it slowly turned to crying as we looked for the lost baby. Mam rushed over and righted the pram and picked Glenys up. Beti and I were not allowed to mind Glenys for some time after that. And that's another problem with grown-ups. If anything goes wrong, they seldom give you a second chance.

I enjoyed going to the cowshed at milking time. I would take with me a cup that Father would fill by milking straight from the cow's teat. This wasn't milk, it was nectar. Once Mari the new maid had finished milking Black-nose, tethered next to Gwenhwyfar the brindle cow, I would be allowed to feed milk to the cats. They would run over towards me, fighting for a place around the dish. Sometimes they would be there before the milk, and I would pour milk and froth over their heads and their ears. Mari would laugh and give me more milk to pour for them.

As usual something came along to disrupt my enjoyment. One night Mari had already filled three-quarters of her milking pail when I asked whether I could try my hand at milking. She let me sit beside her on a stool. She told me to hold one of the cow's teats and squeeze gently and slowly. The cow, unused to my close presence, kicked out. The bucket flew one way and I flew in the opposite direction into the slurry. I was dragged to the house and washed in the bath. And that was the end of my cowshed adventures. It was Mari's fault. Had she let me milk Cochen, the red cow, everything would have been fine. Cochen liked me and she never kicked.

When I returned to school after the summer holidays everything had changed. I was made to sit at a desk next to Charles Cornwal. And I was expected to learn things. Charles remained a close friend in later life and Father employed him for a while. One day Miss Rees, the headmistress, set us a task. She asked us to form a sentence that included the word 'farmer'. Charles came up with a classic,

'The farmer is a beautiful man in his Sunday best.'

His reward was a clip around the ear. Today I can well appreciate Charles' sentiments.

The school curriculum was based on the 'Three Rs', Reading, 'Riting and 'Rithmetic. These were our staple diet other than at playtime. I hated reading, as Miss Davies would always insist on sitting next to me. She would run her index finger along the lines on the pages. Her ample backside would fill the desk, pushing me into the corner and stifling me. Even worse was the fact that the books were boring. But even worse than that was the sickly overpowering odour that hung over Miss Davies, making me want to cough. Much later in life I was looking through some clothes in a cupboard in the old house. And there it was. It was the smell of mothballs.

The school had no playground. But as it stood on abbey land, Father would allow Miss Rees to let us play down by the river. Wintertime, and the river Teifi frozen over, we would skate on its surface. Sometimes one of the girls would fall and slide on her backside, ripping the seat of her knickers. The ice would also allow us to cross the river and wander along to the former lead-washing ponds at the old Bronberllan mines. We would skate there as well until Miss Rees' shrill blast of the whistle summoned us back to school. Today I can appreciate how dangerous it all was. Fortunately, we managed to return without harm every time.

On our way to the river we would pass the school toilets. The boys' toilets were on the school side and the girls' on the opposite side. Should there be a fight between two of the boys, we would all move out of sight of the teachers to the toilet yard. On one occasion there was an altercation between William Tŷ'n Cwm and myself over the ownership of a conker we found on the playground. The matter had to be sorted out in the toilet yard. We fought hammer and tongs until the school bell rang. We returned to the classroom to the cheering of the rest of the pupils. William's nose was bloodied and I had a loose tooth. One of the girls reported us to Miss Rees and we both received a clout each to add to our existing injuries. It proved once again that you can never trust girls to keep anything to themselves!

4

Schooldays and Stallions

ANOTHER BABY ARRIVED in our house. But this time my parents had been wise enough to request a boy. They named him David, but we all called him Dai, an easy name to pronounce. I was now Beti's minder. I took her with me to school every day. She would be fine until we reached the door. Then she would turn around and try and run back home. But I would be too quick for her. I would shove her into the lobby where, once spotted by Miss Rees, she wouldn't stand a chance.

Around this time Miss Davies retired. For some strange reason no one came to take her place so Miss Rees had to cope with us all. The school comprised of only one room, split along the middle. In the far end there was a coal fire that would be lit every morning by either Lizzie or Ann Oliver, or to us Lisi and Ann Olfir. The two sisters acted as caretakers throughout my time at school. They would always ensure that the coal bucket was full so that Miss Rees could feed the fire and keep it going all day. Sometimes the senior children would be allowed to do this, using brass tongs that hung next to the fender.

On one side of the room there were three windows looking

out over the cemetery and another window in the opposite wall looking out over our garden. Sometimes we would see Jack Sais or Gordon pushing a wheelbarrow full of weeds and I would wave to them while the other children laughed. Gordon was a poet. He used to jot down verses on the back of the loosebox door, some of them rather crude. In fact, a few of them can still be seen.

At the back end of the classroom was the shed where the bier was kept. It was used to carry the coffins of dead people at funerals. But every time there was a funeral we would be given the afternoon off. We didn't like funerals because everyone there looked sad, but we enjoyed our time off.

After Miss Davies had left, Miss Rees would cross the divide between the two classes in turn. She used two blackboards, one for the infants and the other for us, the upper form. She was very cunning. Sometimes, when she had her back to me, I would take the opportunity to pinch Charles Cornwal. But even when she looked the other way she would see me. Even when she played the piano at singing practice and had her back to us all, she knew exactly who was singing and who wasn't. I hated singing. But every time I stopped she would turn around and ask me sharply,

'Why aren't you singing?'

I would only blush and say nothing. I didn't dare tell her that my Uncle Siencyn would always tell me,

'Charles, you'll never make a singer. You are an elocutionist.'

Gradually even she realised I couldn't sing, and during singing lessons she would give me other important things to do such as clearing the books from the desks or wiping the blackboard clean while the rest continued singing around the piano. The singing lesson would always be the last lesson every afternoon before we were allowed to go home. And we would all count the minutes – especially when the weather was fine – for the moment that Miss Rees would release us. We would be out of the door even before she had finished telling us we could go.

Before long my little sister Glenys began attending. She started by just attending in the afternoons. But I had a job persuading her to come home with me and Beti. She loved playing with clay and other playthings. One day, towards the end of July as I was dragging her home, I saw by the corner of the workshop the most beautiful horse I had ever seen. It was in the middle of the road impatiently pawing the ground with its hooves, its metal shoes spraying sparks. Then it neighed and playfully tried to bite the arm of its rider who was chatting to my father, neither of them taking any notice of the stallion's antics.

I knew immediately that this was the kind of horse I would ride one day. He was a fine-looking stallion, his body roan with four white legs, the whiteness riding high up on his hind legs. Above his fetlocks the white hair was also long and curly. He had a white patch on his forehead right down to his muzzle and his underbelly was also white. From his tail up and along his rump ran a strap that connected with another strap around his middle. The bridle around his head was decorated with brass buckles. Tied to the strap on his back was a small sack. It looked similar to the sacks that my father received every spring containing swede seeds. It was the kind of sack in which Ifan John who lived in Lisburne Row used to carry his ferret.

There I was, observing the stallion, with Beti and Glenys

impatiently waiting. My father, as usual, broke the spell by ordering me to take the girls to the house. Mam told me that the man on horseback was Dafydd Rees from Penuwch and that his stallion was called Brenin Gwalia. Mr Rees became a regular caller, bringing other cob stallions. But not one of them was anything like Brenin Gwalia.

Soon I had two pretend horses of my own. I would ride one and lead the other. Sometimes Davies the Ruins would see me and ask,

'Where are you taking the stallion today?'

And I would always answer, 'To Abergwesyn, of course!'

I would gladly have left school back then to follow a stallion. But every time I asked Mam why I had to go to school day after day, her answer was always the same,

'So that you can learn to read, write and add up sums and perhaps one day you will go to college.'

Obviously Mam knew very little about school because Miss Rees wanted me to act, draw pictures, dance, do physical training, perform in concerts and other useless activities. I once told Miss Rees that Mam only wanted me to read, write and do add up sums. Her response was to clout me on the back. I never told her again what Mam wanted me to do.

It was just before the end of the summer term when Miss Rees came in one day with a collection of band instruments. She intended taking three-quarters of the pupils to the village carnival. For a fortnight my friend Charles Cornwal and I practised on the drums. We were hitting the drums so hard that the paint was flaking off the metal. One day, we were marched up and down the path alongside the river, all of us drumming or playing our instruments. Come the day of the carnival and everything was arranged. Miss Rees took the infants in her car while we the older children were taken by Ieuan Pantyfedwen in his car. We were to meet by the monument and then change our clothes in the church hall. We were given uniforms made of paper. As he got dressed, Dai Tom's foot tore his trouser leg and it had to be replaced. We all stood there to attention waiting for Miss Rees' command. Charles and I had our drums strapped on and we were dressed in our colourful paper suits. From my shoulder down to my knees I wore a leopard-skin design. Off we marched to the Red Lion yard where the vicar stood on the wall shouting orders through a megaphone. We, the band, were to lead the parade. And on command, off we set to cheers and shouts of encouragement. Dick John lost his tambourine before we had even crossed the bridge. Worse was to come. As we reached Evan Hughes' shop it started raining. By the time we reached halfway up Terrace Road, all I had on to cover my birthday suit was my drum and my underpants. Then it was back again to the monument and then into the hall to change back to our own clothes. The rain literally put a damper on the carnival and that was the first and last time we had a school band. It was also the last village carnival for some time as the Second World War put a stop to it.

The next scholastic year began with a visit from a doctor and nurse who had come to inject us. The cowpox injection left its scar on our upper arms. As we were all sat in the same room it began a war of nerves, each of us waiting to see who would be the first to cry. A few of the girls did and one or two of the boys yelped. Milwyn very nearly let out a swearword almost clear enough for Miss Rees to hear him. I was wearing a jumper and I had to take it off, as well as my shirt. The nurse held my head firmly against the back of my chair. I felt like a pig on slaughter day with Alf, the senior manservant, holding the pig's head steady for Uncle Morgan to plunge the knife into its neck. I was on the verge of bawling but I bit my lip and held out. We were all given a comforting cup of tea afterwards and allowed out to play by the river. But we were all too painful to play so we just sat down and moped. Ifan Defi Bronberllan started rolling around on the ground. He rolled too far and fell over the bank and into the river. He was away from school for two days and when he came back he was boasting that it had all been a stunt so that he could skive off school.

This was around the time when Miss Rees started preparing food for us at midday. We were asked to provide our own plates, bowls and cutlery. We didn't have a cook or a proper kitchen. Miss Rees would prepare the food during our morning playtime. Mam would often provide a cut of meat and vegetables served with mashed potatoes. Often we would have corned beef. When we had *cawl* or Welsh broth I would always use a basin I received as a present from my grandmother. It was white with red and yellow flowers. Unfortunately, the *cawl* would always be piping hot. One day, Charles and I took our basins out and placed them in the nearby brook so that the *cawl* would cool off. In the cold water our basins cracked and the *cawl* disappeared with the flow. That day we had to go without dinner, although William Tŷ'n Cwm slipped me a potato under the table.

As I grew older I had to learn more advanced knowledge and was given homework daily. As I lived so close to the school I was at a distinct disadvantage. If Miss Rees wasn't happy with my work she would call to complain to Mam. Every morning, following the headmistresses' inspection of our homework, we were given a subject to write about and were expected to complete at least ten lines before she came around again. Charles' writing was all over the place. But it was a premeditated plan. By writing so untidily he knew that Miss Rees wouldn't be able to decipher what he had written about or whether his spelling was correct. Her favourite form of punishment was to keep us in at morning playtime and force us to do girls' tasks such as peeling potatoes or stir the *cawl*. Once would normally be enough. None of us boys wanted to suffer such humiliation.

Often, at playtime, Twm Factory would arrive outside on his bike. Twm lived in the village and was mentally unstable. We would watch him through the window as he jumped in and out of the river. Sometimes he would offer us a ride on his bike, only to snatch it back and clean it with his handkerchief. Miss Rees would sometimes come out and send Twm on his way. Twm merely moved away a short distance and rode his bike round and round.

He then would creep into the cemetery and stare at us through the school window. We would laugh at his antics. Every time Miss Rees turned to look, Twm would duck out of sight. Another stunt was to hide behind the gravestones. He became more and more of a nuisance and the school door had to be kept locked just in case. He then took to jumping over the garden wall and peering in through the window, playing hide-and-seek. We would follow his antics and shout to Miss Rees,

'There he is, Miss! He's now at the other window!'

This was one of the funniest periods of my schooldays.

Twm kept us entertained. But, as usual, the good times came to an end. Twm disappeared suddenly and we never saw him again. I believe he was sent to a mental hospital.

Twm was a far more welcome visitor than the schools' dentist. He was a short, ginger-haired little man who seemed full of himself. He would be accompanied by a spindly-legged nurse, her face plastered with make-up. The older boys would help bring in the big chair and equipment. Dick John would sometimes grab a pair of pincers and use it to pinch the girls in a rather delicate part of their anatomy. We would be called in turn to sit there sweating in the chair. Looking up, I would always be surprised by the dentist's own yellow teeth.

Whoever was in the horrid chair would be the centre of our attention. As long as it was someone else in the chair, we would be happy. I remember Henry Tŷ Ucha waiting for the awful injection. He returned to his desk, awaiting the dreaded call for the extraction to take place. We laid bets that he would cry. But no. It became a battle between the dentist and Henry's tooth. The dentist tugged and pulled but the tooth was unmoving. Henry bravely refrained from crying. After a prolonged battle, a tooth the size of a ram's incisor rattled in the aluminium bowl held by the nurse. That evening Henry's mother discovered that the red-headed sadist had extracted a perfectly healthy tooth. The bad tooth was still there!

Years later I recalled the incident to Dai Caemadog. He, in turn, remembered the time his brother Ianto went to the Cross Inn pub in Ffair Rhos, where Nicholas the dentist held a weekly surgery. According to Dai, his brother had a rotten tooth with roots like an oak tree. Nicholas clamped his pincers around the offending tooth. Ianto, said Dai, was pulled three times around the bar before the tooth was extracted. When asked how much Nicholas had charged him, Ianto said he was trembling to such an extent that he couldn't reach for his money. So the dentist had to help himself and take the appropriate payment from Ianto's pocket.

5

War and Peace

ONE DAY, A new girl came to school. Miss Rees welcomed her and described her as what I understood to be a *'faciwî'*. What in the world was a *'faciwî'*? It turned out that she was an evacuee. She was given a desk in the front, right next to the blackboard. Miss Rees explained that the new girl was from London but, because German bombs were dropping there, she had come to live among us. She didn't have a word of Welsh and she had a strange name. I knew of many girls named Ann or Annie but this girl was called Anna.

She became a nuisance, always asking Charles and I the meaning of Welsh words and phrases. We could just about understand her questions, but trying to give her an answer in English was another matter completely. We wondered why the government couldn't send us Welsh-speaking evacuees. Ifan Bronberllan told Miss Rees loud and clear that if it was the other way round and our school was in danger of being bombed, he would refuse point-blank to go to London. Later, more evacuees arrived in the area, most of them from Liverpool. One came to stay with my grandmother. But he attended the village school at Pontrhydfendigaid because it was nearer. I went to visit grandma the following Saturday and ate the nicest food I had ever tasted. Brian's mother – yes, his name was Brian – had sent him a tin of baked beans and he and I ate the lot.

One of the most important people in the area at the time was Rhys Jones the Postman. Rhys had been in the First World War and knew of every battlefield and trench in Europe. He would call at our house every dinnertime when he would tell us where the Germans were located at the time. Sometimes he would draw a map on the back of an envelope to show where the present battles were being fought. He knew the names of towns and villages in France and Holland and I would repeat these names to my friends at school. Should we be playing by the river when Rhys called he would, with the end of his walking stick, draw a map of Europe in the gravel. He would then fill in the boundaries of the various countries and then place stones here and there to show us where the Germans had broken through.

Rhys would also describe dramatically the big guns and the effect their booming noise had on the soldiers. Unfortunately, he wouldn't be able to linger very long as he was expected to walk his lengthy mountainous route delivering mail. He would start from the village, calling in at all the farms and cottages in the Glasffrwd valley. Then he would aim for Pen Bwlch, the highest point, and cross the river Tywi seven times before reaching Moel Prysgau. He would then bear right over the mountain to Garreg Lwyd and back down through Cwm Moiro to Penddolfawr and then follow the river Teifi back to the village. Sometimes we would be leaving school by the time he returned to collect mail from the post box that was in the school wall, and we would urge him to tell us more tales.

Charles and I realised that the more often we talked to

Anna, the better our English became. There was no one else around we could talk to in English except Jack Sais. Rhys the Postman would warn us against talking to strangers, be they English or Welsh in case they were German spies. At playtimes, we would – the boys and the girls – march up and down along the riverbank. Occasionally we would divide into two armies and train, so that we would know what to do when called up to join the army.

At the end of May 1942, the war came to us. There was a gang of farm workers, those from Pantyfedwen and our lads, Alf and George, on Pen Bwlch cutting peat ready for harvesting later for the coming winter. They were stacking the turfs in piles of six on the bank to dry. They heard the sound of an approaching plane from the direction of Gynnon Lake. They could tell from the groaning noise of its engines that something was amiss. They all jumped into the peat furrows and took cover as they thought it was a German plane. It suddenly appeared over the bank, coughing and spluttering barely ten feet above ground. Within seconds it plunged into the peatbog between Graig Wen and Pen Bwlch. For weeks, air force officials worked at dismantling what remained of the Wellington and moved the larger sections away. The bodies of the three crew were found. The smaller parts of the plane are still to be seen up there.

Later, when there was no one around, I would go up there and look for bits of metal or Perspex. I would then take the smaller pieces and show them off in school. Dai Tom warned me that, if the authorities found out, I would be taken and placed against the barn wall and shot as a spy. I believed him and considered running away to hide somewhere.

One day, as I arrived home from school, I thought the end

had come. In the kitchen there were three uniformed soldiers talking to Father. I crept silently upstairs and waited until they had left in their army jeep. When I eventually ventured down I discovered that they were three GIs and that Father had rented two of his fields to them, Cae Grîn (Green Field) as a base for small planes, and Cae Gwair (Hay Field) as a camping base. Part of the meadow by the river had also been earmarked for storing petrol.

Not long afterwards a lorry-load of GIs arrived to start work on erecting the camp. Part of Cae Gwair's hedgebank was cleared away as an entrance for the tanks and lorries, and markings were placed here and there to denote the positions of the tents. Two soldiers examined the surface of Cae Grîn to ensure that there were no hidden dangers, such as rocks or stones, that could affect the take-offs and landings of planes. My father was then warned of the impending arrival of the troops, vehicles and equipment. It would be on the coming Tuesday. Dick, Charles and I decided that we would, after tea on arrival day, go to Dôl Coed field to watch the troops arriving. Our fields stretched on each side of the road almost as far as the village. They were lined with hazel trees, a good place to hide and watch the road. We hid in a hazel bush, sitting there for a good hour. Then we heard the sound of engines in the distance. A few minutes later the first lorry appeared over Glasffrwd bridge. Soon the road was filled with lorries, tanks, jeeps and then more lorries, with clouds of dust hovering over everything. We hid there among the branches, too scared to move. As the lorries passed we could see helmeted soldiers. To us they looked like German soldiers. Dick swore he had heard some of them speaking German and this made us even more frightened. We didn't dare move until the last vehicle had long disappeared. Then we crept home across the fields.

Within a few days the locals became used to seeing military men and vehicles and Dick, Charles and I were introduced to chewing gum. Every day on the farm we could hear the tanks firing, the noise reverberating, scaring the shire horses in the stable and putting them off their food, in particular Lester, the bay mare. Alf was afraid of clearing away her dung in case she kicked him.

The chassis and body of an old car had been placed up on Moel Prysgau as a target for the guns to aim at. For years afterwards the peatbog was pitted with shell holes. Sometimes the soldiers would go on manoeuvres dressed in camouflage. They would divide into two groups, one trying to capture the other. Sometimes, when Charles and I looked for rabbits in Cwm Crogant, we would discover soldiers hiding there. On one occasion, as we were following the river Glasffrwd, we came across two soldiers with their arms around two village women. We crept away and when we got back to the farm I told Mam what I had seen. I told her the soldiers were keeping the women captive. Mam ignored me and gave us an apple each and sent us out to play.

The best time to visit the camp was on a Sunday night. The camp shop would be open and Dick, Charles and I would queue with the soldiers. We never had any money but we would always be given chewing gum all the same. We would then creep around the camp and aim for the big tent where films were shown. With the canvas held down by wooden pegs, it would be an easy task to pull up a peg and slide in beneath the canvas. From there we could see the screen. We seldom saw a cowboy film. No, most of the films showed women wearing next to nothing. Dick thought America was a very hot place if women could go around with nothing much on! Slowly our eyes would get used to the darkness inside, just the beam of the projector lighting the place. In its glow we would see rows of faces. Among them we could recognise one or two faces of women from the village. They must have been able to buy tickets, we thought.

One Sunday night – the three of us lying there and watching – a large soldier tripped over us creating a bit of a commotion. In the wink of an eye we were out from under the canvas and up and running through Bronberllan's front field. After that we never went to the pictures again in case we'd be caught and shot.

Among all the American vehicles the most interesting were the small two-seater planes that were forever taking off and landing on Cae Grîn. Sometimes, with Charles, Dick and I wandering along the slopes above Cwm Crogant woods, a plane would fly so low that we had to duck and sometimes lie flat on the ground. We would be able see the pilot clearly in his cockpit. We kept pestering the pilot, begging him to take us for a trip in the plane. But he would always make excuses. But things took an unexpected turn.

One day, Charles and I were sitting on the stone steps leading to the loft above the cart house when we heard someone calling to us from the neighbouring field. It was the pilot. Earlier that day he had lost his watch somewhere around there and he asked us to help him look for it. We joined him and the watch was found. He gave us a white packet of chewing gum to share between us. But we pointed at the plane and tried to persuade him again to take us up. And this time we were soon in the plane, strapped in the seat behind the pilot. He fired the engine and then the plane was careering along the grass like a demented pheasant. Up we rose and I dared to look down. We were flying towards Tregaron bog. I could see the village beneath, Terrace Road and the Square. The river was just a ribbon. We could see Ystrad Meurig to the right and the railway running like an arrow through the bog. We were now heading left and, as we crossed Tregaron, the pilot said something but I only understood the word 'home'. I was glad. By now I was convinced he was going to take us somewhere across the sea and not come back. I could feel tears welling in my eyes and Charles' face was ashen. Over Tregaron he took a turn but I wasn't looking down any longer. From the corner of my eye I could see we were flying over mountainous heathland and I recognised Bryneithinog. And then the abbey arch came into view. We circled the field and soon we were down once more on solid ground. Charles and I never asked the pilot again for a trip in his plane.

The senior farmhand was Alf and he was in charge of the horses. He joined the village Home Guard, and soon he knew everything about capturing Germans. They would arrive at night, he said, dropping from parachutes. The Home Guard would meet every Sunday for manoeuvres on a nearby meadow. They would form two squads. One would pretend to occupy a position held by Germans, with the other trying to capture it. One day they were practising a fire drill and pumping water from the river. The hose became loose and the water spouted like a fountain, sending Dick Rees flying up in the air!

Sometimes Alf would come into the kitchen wearing his uniform, his black boots shining. He wore short leggings above his ankles and, as I watched him leaving on his Raleigh bicycle, I felt so jealous of him. Most of the men were middle-aged and older, and Dick, Charles and I hoped the war wouldn't end before we were old enough to join the Home Guard.

Although the Americans were firing their big guns daily, Miss Rees would be reluctant for us to lose even one school day. We were not allowed to play by the river any more as the petrol store was nearby, meaning that there was a constant movement of lorries, jeeps and motorbikes. So at playtime we were confined to the classroom.

One of our farmhands at the time was Rod Glangorsfach. He was in charge of the cows. Following feeding and milking they would be turned out to the Lan above the farm. It meant that Rod would be passing the petrol store four times daily. Normally it would be unattended. Tom, Rod's brother, owned a motorbike and found it difficult to obtain the necessary petrol coupons. He asked Rod to help himself to a petrol can. They were large, flat containers. Rod decided to try and open a can to see if it was full. It was a warm day and, unbeknown to him, he had opened a high-octane can of aeroplane fuel. As he opened the can, the fuel shot into his face. Poor Rod was half-blinded and his brother had to go without the illicit petrol.

Despite the disruption caused by the war even in our quiet little retreat, Miss Rees would still take us out after dinner to gather moss in the woods beyond the river Glasffrwd. The older boys would carry the moss back in bags and store it in a heap behind our barn, with Father's permission. Miss Rees told us that the moss would later be sent to war zones to be placed on the wounds of injured soldiers. Miss Rees always emphasised to us the importance of defeating Hitler and how we could all play our part. This would spur us on to collect more and more moss, even if it was raining.

Every time a local soldier would come home on leave, especially should there be three or four home at the same time, a concert would be organised in the church hall with the proceeds going to the soldiers. I would look forward to these events. Father would take me, Beti and Glenys there. We would walk the mile there and back, everywhere in total darkness because of the blackout over every window in every home. The concert compère was Jack Oliver, the barber from Ffair Rhos. He was full of jokes and would make us laugh out loud with his conjuring tricks.

Top of the bill would be a duo from Cross Hands, Sioni and Iori. They would sing songs making fun of Hitler. During the interval the returned soldier would appear on the stage. We would all clap. Our family would clap even harder if Uncle Jack or Uncle Will were among those on leave. I had to poke Glenys in the ribs to remind her to clap. Little girls, unlike us boys, didn't realise how brave these men were.

One of the worst sights I witnessed back then was to see hundreds of soldiers going past. They had been up in the hills of Tywi and Moel Prysgau and were looking bedraggled. One day I came home to see Dr Davies from Tregaron, together with an important-looking officer, talking to Mam at the back door. Mam explained later that the doctor had been called out to attend to some of these soldiers who were suffering from exposure. They were to be marched down past our house the following day and then taken by lorry to a camp where the conditions would be considerably better. Mam was busy baking bread all day and I was kept from school the following day to help Mam, Father and Mat the maid feed these men as they awaited transport. One soldier who was suffering with bad feet gave me a penknife. It was late evening by the time we finished feeding them.

The war ended for me on Caemadog meadow. I was walking home having been visiting an aunt. Who came to meet me wearing a long khaki coat but Uncle Jack. It was a warm day and I was wearing a sleeveless shirt. Mam told me later that Uncle Jack had just returned from a place called Burma and I was warned not to ask him anything about the war. Suddenly, the summer and the school holidays were over and soon I would have far more important matters to deal with.

6

The Young Farmer

I WAS TEN years old and by now the oldest of five children, three of them girls. Girls don't usually make good playmates. But Glenys, the second of my sisters, was just as good as any boy at shinning up trees and she would follow me everywhere. Glenys was good at upsetting people and she and I would sometimes have to make ourselves scarce. Our garden, once a part of the abbey, was a great place to play in. Our gardener was Gordon. Every spring he would dig, plant and sow.

Gordon was a quiet man who preferred to keep his own company. As a poet he won quite a few eisteddfod chairs. He would seldom mix with us children. Glenys' favourite trick was to hide behind the box bushes waiting for Gordon to turn his back. She would then creep out and pull up whatever he had just planted and then run back and hide. Gordon would know full well what was going on but he would never get angry. He would rather try to reason with her, but to no avail.

Another of her hiding places was the elder tree, its branches overhanging the outside toilet. We didn't have an indoor toilet. There were hidden pathways leading to the outside privy. The wall of the ruins ran along one side and the garden hedge on the other. In summer, with the trees in full leaf, it was like walking through a tunnel. Sometimes, with Glenys and I hiding among the branches, Father would enter the toilet. Some six inches had been cut from the top of the toilet door to let in some light. From our perch, some six feet away, we could see whoever was in there. We would watch Father sitting there contentedly smoking his pipe. Often we couldn't help but laugh out loud. Should he hear us we would have to clamber down and run, with Father chasing us swinging his leather belt. Glenys would sometimes be so impetuous in jumping down that she would sometimes leave a piece of her knickers on a branch. Father was quick on his feet and his leather strap would leave red weals on our legs.

Being that toys were at a premium in those days, we improvised. We would look out for anything that could be used in our play. One day, as Charles Cornwal and I were exploring the old coach house, we discovered a crateful of empty lemonade bottles. There was a glass marble lodged in the necks of all the bottles. We smashed the bottles and played with the marbles.

No child was worth knowing if he or she didn't own an iron hoop and a fashioned length of wire to guide it along the road. After much pleading, my father eventually asked Isaac the Blacksmith to forge a hoop for me. It was more exciting that having a new car.

I remember one day the river Teifi in full flood. And, by the side of the river, we discovered the wheel of a chaffing machine. It was made of iron and as big as a cartwheel. It was extremely heavy but we managed to drag it up to the top of the Lan, the high hill behind the house. It took us the best part of four school dinner hours to drag it up there. Having done so, we raised it on its rim and let it go. I can see it now bounding down the slope, leaving a trail as it cut a swathe through the bracken and the gorse like a scythe and headed for the road. We realised, too late, that Tommy the Postman was on his bike on his round and was passing just below the hill. Luckily for us, and even luckier for Tommy, the wheel, as it careered towards him, hit a stone and bounded over him. He never even saw it. And that was that until Father found it half-buried in the field beyond the road.

Gradually, my playing hours grew shorter as my responsibilities on the farm slowly took over. While I was at my father's beck and call, my mother was forever calling me in to finish my homework. The dreaded Scholarship was fast approaching. How I hated being upstairs in my room studying while I could hear the others out at play.

This was a time when Mam was convalescing following a fall. She fell off a chair a few days before my youngest sister was born. Mam spent some time in hospital. The new baby was named Eluned which, over time, was shortened to Luned and later to Lyn. This time I was mostly spared the task of tending her, as Beti and Glenys were now old enough to share the duties. I have often been told that Lyn resembles me. She strongly denies that!

Because of Mam's condition, Father had to take over some of the household duties as we didn't have a maid at the time and I was now quite busy on the farm. At breakfast time Father was driven to despair as he tried to wash and dress some of us and feed us all. One day, Glenys and I sent him berserk as we utilised the black-and-white chequered oilcloth table cover as a draughts board and used bits of cheese as draughts pieces. We were getting on fine until he caught us. I was sent to school that morning with no breakfast.

It was around then that help was needed at milking time. I would help with the milking before leaving for school. I started with the little cow in the middle stall opposite the cowshed door. Named Cochen, the Red One, she was old and docile, perfect for a beginner. Before long I would manage milking three cows every morning before school. After Cochen I would milk Gwenhwyfar, the brindle cow, and then a cow Father had bought from Dai the Tailor from Ffair Rhos. She wasn't with us for very long. One day, she was out on the Back Field where Mam hung out the washing. By the time Mam had arrived to take in the clothes, the cow had eaten half the washing. On the following Tuesday she was for sale at Tregaron mart!

Before too long I did not have to pick and choose; I could milk any of the cows. The cowshed in winter was a good place to be. As I milked I could feel the caress of the cow's hair on my cheek. But in summer I hated the work, especially when the cows had nits. During hay harvest time I would milk half the herd myself. By the time I finished I felt like Guy Fawkes, with my arms hanging limply at my sides.

I always looked forward to the hay harvest. The weather tended to be fine and it coincided with the school holidays. My job would be to look after my sisters and brother. I was warned to keep them away from the fields and the machinery. My favourite playground would be Cae Bach or Small Field next to the rickyard where the grey pony, Llwyden, the Gray One, would be kept. The pony would be ridden regularly by Father or one of the farmhands. Between the five of us we would easily catch it. I could manage, if I stood on tiptoe, to fit the bridle over its head and then lead it to a large stone on which I could stand and make it easier for us to mount the pony, all five of us. We would fall off quite regularly, especially when Llwyden decided to canter.

One day, with all the adults busy in Cae Gwair, we decided to ride over there. Everything was fine until Alf and the black mare came along, towing the hay shaker. The mare would half-canter while the shaker shook the hay, scattering it in all directions like autumn leaves blown by the wind. Llwyden took fright and galloped across the field. I had to let go of the reins and grab her mane, but to no avail. Beti slipped down under Llwyden's belly, dragging the rest of us with her. We were never allowed to enter Cae Gwair on Llwyden afterwards, and the mare became wary of any haymaking machines.

The chore I hated the most was churning. We had a large churn anchored to the dairy floor. It was connected by means of a spindle to a turning device we referred to as a gearing that had two cogged wheels working in conjunction. Then, connected to the gearing was a long wooden shaft. The shaft was then attached to Flower, the grey horse, who walked around in a circle thus turning the gearing and therefore the churn. My job was to lead the horse round and round until the cream had gradually coagulated into butter. Yellow blobs of butter could be seen floating on the surface of the milk, or by now buttermilk. Having led the horse for so long round the gearing, I would feel quite drunk.

Having stabled Flower I would return to the dairy where Mam would have a glassful of buttermilk waiting for me. Sometimes I would take a jugful out to share between the men, especially on warm days. Mam would then spend an hour curing the butter. Most would be put in a large earthenware pot, while the rest would be shaped into blocks.

The blocks would then be decorated with various designs using a flat wooden device that looked like a table tennis bat but with a pattern carved into it. There were various shapers with different designs. We would sometimes take the moulds and sneak out and pretend to make butter out of mud. Woe betides us should Mam catch us.

Another chore I always tried to avoid was helping Alf on Saturday mornings to chop logs for the wall oven where Mam would bake bread and cakes. The oven in the wash house was large enough to take fifteen large loaves and two slabs of cake. Before baking, the oven had to be heated. It would be filled with logs. These were then set alight until the surrounding bricks that lined the oven were red-hot. The ashes would then be raked out and the tins containing the dough would be placed inside to bake.

One Saturday morning I was halfway up the oak tree in the Back Field when Alf called me to help him to saw some tree trunks. I hated the long saw that needed two to use it, one at each end pulling it back and forth. The handle always hurt my hand. I must have lost my rhythm, causing the toothed blade to jump out of its groove and leave a deep cut on Alf's hand. Blood was pouring out of the wound. I ran to the house for help and out came the maid, Mat, to see what all the fuss was about. Alf had to be taken to the doctor to have the wound stitched. Alf, much to his credit, never blamed me and we continued sawing together for years to come.

The corn harvest was an important event. When the sheaves were dry enough to be brought in, Father would ask Miss Rees to release me from school to help with the loading. Two flat carts would be used to bring in the loads of corn. These carts were known as 'gambos', and while one was being unloaded in the rickyard the other was being loaded in the field.

Alf and Jack would pitch the sheaves onto the gambo where Father would receive them. And woe betides us if a sheaf landed behind him. The sheaves, as they were being unloaded, would be placed on top of each other to form a rick. Father would keep a sharp eye, ensuring that the rick would be perfectly formed. Sometimes Dai Cornwal would happen to be passing. He would stay to watch, shouting out his advice,

'Out a little, Tom. You need pulling in a bit on the next layer.'

I looked forward to the day when I would be allowed to build a rick from the ground all the way up to the top. There were three reasons why I loved the corn harvest. One, it meant missing school. Two, I would be allowed to wear long trousers to avoid my knees being stung by thistles. And three, when the last load would be brought in I would be allowed to sit on top of it making the school pupils jealous of me as we passed by. Sometimes, though, if the thistles were particularly abundant, my long trousers would be useless. My knees would be stung so badly that I would have a problem walking for days afterwards.

By the end of the harvest there would be eight ricks in the yard. After they had settled we would thatch their tops with reeds to keep them as dry as possible over the winter. The men would go up to Dolbeudiau bog with a scythe each to cut the reeds and bring them home in a gambo. The reeds would first be sorted on the stable floor. The men would grab a bunch and shake it to get rid of any grass. The longest reeds would be used to cap the rick. Anything left would then be twisted into long ropes to tie down the cap.

Making these ropes wasn't pleasant work. And, usually, I would have to undertake that work. It would involve using a simple device: a piece of wire and two elder sticks. The wire would be looped around the sticks and a hook on one end. My job was to keep turning this device while my father fed in the reeds until the rope stretched the length of the stable. These lengths would run around a foot apart, holding down the reed covering on top. These ropes would also be tied around the ricks from the base to the top.

This was a frustrating time for me on the farm, with so many other interesting activities happening regularly. But I would only be asked to help. Yet I knew I could be as good as anyone if given the chance.

The last Saturday in April was always an important day. That was when the sheep would be rounded up to be marked before being driven to spend the summer on the mountain. Father would be joined at the entrance to Talwrn by Dai Morgan Grofftau. They would leave with their dogs, heading for the woods and Waun Wen. Hearing their shouts as they reached the river, Alf, Jack and I would join them to help drive the young lambs across the river. On reaching the river they tended to turn back and scatter. We would scare them into turning round, by shouting, whistling and flapping our overcoats. Despite our efforts, some half-dozen would always manage to escape to the woods. Father, however, would praise the men. I would be standing there red-faced, sweating and out of breath.

After that we would all sit down to breakfast at the farmhouse before gathering the sheep from the Lan and the surrounding fields. They would then be herded in Cae Bach and taken in groups to the cart house. Alf, Jack and I would do the catching, while Father cut notches in their ears – a split in the left ear and cutting off the tip of the right ear. Dai Morgan would then punch a hole in the right ear before marking them all with red dye above their tails. The male lambs would be herded together in the loosebox and would not be marked until later.

Dai Phillips Llwyngog was in charge of the lambs that were to be castrated. He would sit on a bench facing Dai Grofftau. First he would use a sharp knife before turning to the pincers. But before that I had to dab a green slimy ointment over the shiny steel instrument. I pleaded and pleaded to be allowed to take over but I was always refused. Dai would ignore me and carry on with the work as if he was deaf.

Once a year Ben Felix from Llanwrtyd would call to castrate the colts. Among those to be dealt with would be riding ponies and shire horses, some of them kicking and jumping around as Father and Alf tried to tether them. I wanted to help, but again I would be ignored. Should I approach too close to the action, Father would scold me. I would retreat and climb onto the chaff box, a good place to watch everything that went on. Ben would chat incessantly as he used bits of hazel wood to stem the flow of blood. Ben secretly promised me that one day he would call when Father was away and allow me to practise. But nothing came of it.

There was another wooden chest nearby with a heavy lid. In it there were all kinds of strange-looking instruments. There were devices for treating the feet of sheep and horses' hooves, a gun for dosing, and a two-handled knife for docking shire horses' tails. The docking was always carried out in the stall opposite the door. This would allow more light for carrying out the task. A collar would be placed over the horse's head and Father would grab it by the muzzle and slowly twist a rope around the horse's nose. This would render the horse unconscious so that it wouldn't feel the knife cutting through the flesh of the tail. In the kitchen there would be long irons in the fire and, when they were red-hot, I would grab them by the handles and rush over to hand them to Father. He would use them to close the wound and stem the flow of blood. Later, the Ministry of Agriculture banned this treatment but the knife is still in the wooden box to remind me of those days of long ago.

7

Cold Comfort

THERE ARE SOME years that linger in the memory and 1947 was a year that will forever stay with me. There are three reasons for this. Firstly, the blizzard that decimated sheep stocks. Secondly, it was the year of the dreaded Scholarship. And thirdly, it was the year when I left the Abbey School for the secondary school six miles away at Tregaron.

It was a Thursday morning in February and, as it started snowing around mid morning, Miss Rees allowed us all to go home. I was delighted. During the afternoon the wind rose, blowing the powdery snow under the door like icing sugar. The following day the Tilley lamps had to be filled with paraffin and lit much earlier than usual as it was darkening.

Usually three lamps were needed, one for the cowshed, one for the stable and the third for the barn. But before we managed to reach any of those they were extinguished by the gale that was now blowing relentlessly. We managed to relight two of the lamps but the third lamp's mantle was in pieces.

When I woke up the following morning my bedroom was completely dark. I thought at first that I had got up far too early. I lay back in bed hoping to go back to sleep. Then I heard voices from downstairs. I lit the candle and went to the window. But I couldn't see a thing. I quickly dressed and went downstairs and then realised what had happened. The front of the house, as high as the roof, was completely covered with snow. There was so much snow that it didn't disappear completely until the last week in June.

I have never seen such snow. The cowshed was almost covered over. There was no sign of the rickyard hedge, and the gate leading to Cae Bach was completely covered. The wind remained strong, blowing snow that was so dense that we couldn't see the Back Field. The men were at it all day clearing what they could of the drifts. They dug a tunnel into the cowshed and then cleared a way for the cows and horses so that they could reach the brook for water. Then they cleared a path to the toilet in the garden. Visiting the toilet was like entering an igloo, and it was so cold that no one would linger there long. The men were so busy with the cows and horses, digging for logs and coal to keep the fire going, releasing the two fatted pigs and the sow, as well as tending to other necessities, that we weren't able to start looking for the sheep until Sunday.

We, the children, were enjoying it all as it meant the school was closed. And we were confident that it would remain closed for some time to come. I busied myself searching for hens caught under the drifted snow. Every time my digging revealed a dead hen, I would take it to the house to show to Mam. I didn't find the Rhode Island Red cockerel until April when the slowly melting snow revealed its body. We had to find a replacement for him. Glenys spent a whole afternoon digging her way to the potato store. She had an incentive, as Mam had promised her – if she was successful – there would be chips for us all that night. Chip night was an event to savour, even under normal circumstances. We would play our part in peeling the potatoes. And what a mad scramble when the chip dish reached the table!

The weekend brought with it a hard frost that froze the tap by the back door. For almost six weeks we had to carry water by the bucketful from the running spring near Cornwal. I overheard my father talking to the men, saying how worried he was about the sheep. Very few could be seen and the snow by now was as hard as concrete. Little did we realise that weekend that half our flock would be lost and that only a tenth of the usual number of lambs would hear the cuckoo that coming spring.

It was impossible to travel the country mile between us and the village as the road was lower than the adjoining fields with the result that drifts reached the tops of the hedges. This merely confirmed my prophecy that the school would be closed for weeks. I was wrong. On Monday morning I was standing on the cart house steps and looking towards the village when I saw three people coming towards me across the fields. I couldn't believe my eyes when I recognised one of them as Miss Rees. She had managed to persuade some council workers to clear a path to the school. The road was passable for the first half a mile but from Glasffrwd bridge onwards the snow was as high as the hedges. Miss Rees therefore had persuaded the men to clear an entrance from near the bridge, allowing her to cross through Dolgoed Field and on across Cae Gwair to school. By dinnertime we were all, together with the Cornwal children, back at school.

Miss Rees was very anxious that I in particular didn't miss school because I would, come spring, have to sit the Scholarship examination. So she doggedly walked all the way to and fro for the six weeks that it took for things to get back to normal. She would wear a long overcoat, and a thick scarf wrapped around her head. I would have given anything for another blizzard, one that would this time keep me from going to school for months.

But now, there I was back at my desk. The school toilet was buried under the snow. Luckily, the coal shed had somehow been spared, so the schoolroom was at least warm. One morning at playtime, as we were out building a snowman, Wag our dog arrived and immediately started scratching in the snow outside the girls' toilet. He was making strange noises exactly as if trying to speak. I ran to fetch my father. When we returned Wag was still at it, scratching and moaning. Father called for Alf and they started clearing away the snow to get to the toilet door. We tried to help as well by carrying away the blocks of freezing snow that Father and Alf were cutting. They reached the door eventually and forced it open. Inside were some four dozen sheep, but only eight were alive. The wind had probably blown the door open and they had crowded in to seek shelter only for the wind to blow it shut again behind them. Snow must have been blown in under the door and through the cracks, stifling most of them. Wag became a hero among us children.

From the beginning of March newborn lambs began to appear, creating a situation that only made things even worse. The lambs, as well as their mothers, were too weak, with one or the other, sometimes both, dying. By mid March we had twenty-one orphaned lambs in the hay shed and it took us a full hour, morning and evening, to feed them with milk and tend them. The female lambs were kept for breeding purposes and, now and then, they must have remembered how they were tended as many would follow me around the field. One of them lived until she was fourteen years old.

I will always remember the snows of 1947, and one incident in particular. There was a huge snowdrift at the bottom end of Dolgoed Field and across the river to Dolebolion heath. There we discovered over five hundred dead sheep. They were not all ours. They had been forced to make their escape down from the hills by the storm. Some had come from as far as the Elan Valley in Radnorshire. Under the weight of the snow, many had been squashed flat. Perhaps the most emotional incident, as far as I was concerned, was when we discovered a newly-bought improved Welsh ram dead in the yew tree marking the grave of Dafydd ap Gwilym in the cemetery. He was hanging from a branch by one of his horns after being tempted there, probably, by the greenery.

The road, as I previously mentioned, from Glasffrwd bridge to the abbey was impassable. And, even after the council workers had cleared a way through, it was almost impossible to remove the blocks of freezing snow they had excavated. As for us, we had to clear an entrance between Cae Bach y Crydd (The Shoemaker's Small Field) and Dôl Teifi, and again between the meadow and Cae Gwair so we could drive the horse and cart to the village to fetch flour for baking bread and foodstuff for the pigs and calves. These entrances were also used to bring bodies of the recently departed from the village to the church. A crew of local men would take it in turns to carry the coffins on their shoulders. And, because the ground was frozen solid, there at the church the coffins had to rest until the thaw. At one time there were as many as eight coffins awaiting burial. There were no JCBs in those days.

As for funerals, I only once witnessed a coffin arriving in a horse-drawn hearse. It was the funeral of Aunty Ann Graigfach. Ifan Hughes Llwyngwyddil's cob was used to draw Dafydd Jenkins' glass-windowed hearse. I remember the black plume that decorated the horse's bridle. Aunty Ann, or Bodo Ann as she was referred to by us children, was related to Mam and I always felt uneasy in her company with her yellowish complexion, long black clothes, and smoking a pipe; and with her lazy black cat with green eyes always by her side in front of the fire. When I later read of Macbeth and the witches, Aunty Ann immediately sprang to mind.

It was the frost of 1947 that pensioned off our watermill. Throughout the big freeze we were unable to use it for chaffing, pulping and milling. I remember the thrill of being allowed to pull the wooden lever that raised the floodgate, letting the water fill the water wheel's paddles. As the paddles filled, the added weight would naturally set the wheel in motion. The wheel then would be connected to a long iron spindle that would, in turn, be attached to one of the implements in the barn. The most awkward of these implements was the chaffing machine. Feeding it with loose straw would often cause it to choke. This would mean cutting off the water flow and reversing the machine, thus freeing it of the blockage.

As the water wheel remained dormant over the freeze, Father bought an oil-driven engine and the rush of water to the pool below the big wheel was stilled. Today I realise I was witness to a slice of history when Father and Will the Coal closed the tailgate of Will's lorry on a rusty old water wheel.

I am often saddened when I recall myself and the other children sitting by the water flume clearing twigs and leaves that threatened to block the water's flow. I would spend nearly an hour in Father's overcoat and gloves ensuring that the wheel's paddles were full of water. Should Dai Cornwal see me, he would warn me that I was courting a dose of pneumonia.

To a twelve year old the snow of 1947 was highly enjoyable. I did not imagine the losses or see Father's bank statement. But Miss Rees was busily forming a cloud above my head. Not a day's schooling passed without my being reminded of the Scholarship. I would be forced to write an essay, a passage in English, and do a bellyful of arithmetic including what she called 'the mentals', fractions and new mathematical problems every day. I soon realised that I was not merely trying to earn my place at Tregaron Grammar School. I was caught in no man's land, in a war between two schools. The war was between the David of our little Abbey School and the Goliath of the large village school in Pontrhydfendigaid. Why the rivalry, I had no idea. But I do remember one incident when we had to join the village school once for the dentist's visit. It led to a battle between us, the boys of the Abbey School and the boys of Pontrhydfendigaid school. That day we all returned home with all our teeth intact. Awarded with the Scholarship locally was a special annual prize, the Princess Sofia Award to whoever from the two schools received the highest marks. And, as far as our school was concerned, I was the lamb being taken to the slaughter.

I remember standing by the Post Office awaiting the school bus that would take me to Tregaron Grammar

School to sit the Scholarship exam. I gazed at Pen-y-Bannau, believing that I would never see the familiar old mountain again. With me was Marina Tŷ'n Cwm, another graduate from the Abbey School who had a desperate look in her eyes. We both had a pencil each, a rubber and a ruler, and looked exactly like two carpenters awaiting the arrival of a body to measure.

Will Lloyd's bus arrived. I jumped on and dumped myself in the nearest empty seat trying to hide my new pair of Holdfast boots. I felt as if everyone's eyes were on me. I don't know about Marina, but I never saw anything on the road to Tregaron. All I knew was that my breakfast was refusing to lie still in my stomach. The walk from the bus to the school hall was like a dream, a bad dream. But I vividly remember my desk against the wall next to the radiator pipes. The first exam paper landed on my desk. These were the dreaded 'mental' sums, twenty sums to be completed within ten minutes. I couldn't have wished for a better start. I completed the task in six minutes. I even shocked myself!

Then disaster. My foot slipped between the radiator pipe and the wall and was stuck. It wouldn't budge. I bent down and tried to remove my boot. Then I heard a voice like thunder from above me,

'Are you cheating, boy?'

I almost failed the Scholarship there and then. I walked out at the end of the afternoon. Never had a twelve-year-old boy appeared to be so old. Back in the village I called at Rhydfen, where Miss Rees lived, to show her the exam papers. Old Mrs Rees, her mother, made me a cup of tea and sandwiches.

A few weeks later I was named winner of the Princess

Sofia Award. I felt like a snail that had cast off its shell. For my last term at the Abbey School I was treated royally by Miss Rees. And, during the following summer holidays, I was allowed to take a greater role and more responsibility on the farm.

One Saturday, with my friend Charles and I kicking our heels, we decided to walk over to Penddolfawr to visit my Uncle Rhys and see what was going on. As we followed the path we could see Uncle Rhys behind a pair of shire horses ploughing Dolau Isaf. We looked for a shallow part of the river where we could cross. When we reached him we pleaded with him to be allowed to hold the reins and follow the plough. Much to our surprise he acceded. I was the first to be given the opportunity of holding the plough handles. I was also allowed to lead the shire horses, the grey workhorse walking the furrow and Teifi, the bay cob walking the fallow. But they were striding too fast for me to follow and, as a result, the furrow was not only crooked but the depth of the plough varied as well. Then it was Charles' turn. Unfortunately, he encountered the same problem. But fair play to Uncle Rhys, he merely laughed. Even today I can see evidence on Dolau Isaf of where my ploughing was too deep. The depressions in the ground have remained over all those years. I wonder if some future archaeologist will one day see those depressions in otherwise level ground and try to decipher what they could have been.

I can't have been all that hopeless. Soon afterwards, Father took me with him to scuffle swedes behind Flower, the grey shire. To begin with, Father told me to walk beside him as he guided Flower up one way and down the other. I studied his every movement as I walked with him. Then, at last, came my turn. I tried emulating my father. I walked behind the scuffler, whispering softly to Flower as Father would always do. I tugged on the line to the right, and Flower responded, moving onto the right hand furrow. Then a stop to ensure that the scuffler was in line behind Flower. And off we set. I was even allowed to turn on the headland. After four successful lengths Father said he needed to return to the farm. Soon he was back with a flask of tea for me as he checked my progress. Then I completed another four lengths. I felt I was quite the man. I looked around, hoping to see some of the neighbours watching me and realising what a head horseman I was. Isn't it strange? When you do something well, especially when you are young, there will be no one there to witness it.

Whatever, as the afternoon wore on I became more confident, indeed overconfident. I was pulling on the lines and shouting commands to Flower. The old mare must have had her fill of all this nonsense. Without any sign of warning, she took off across the furrows still dragging the scuffler. I shouted louder and pulled harder on the lines, but to no avail. She didn't stop until she reached the gate. And that's where Father found us when he arrived with more tea. He wasn't very happy and the tea tasted rather bitter. But, as time passed and I had learnt my lesson, the old mare and I became soulmates.

With the summer fast approaching and the pressure from Miss Rees having lessened considerably, there was more time for farming and also for play in the evenings and on weekends. One memorable event was my first visit to the annual sheep wash. It meant five farms coming together to the washing place at Tywi. There, a pool would be formed by damming the river. This had to be done every year, as the winter floods would invariably wash away the previous year's dam. Some of the men would cut turfs, while others gathered stones from the riverbed and then placed them, turfs and stones, in layers across the river. The turfs and stones were ferried to the site on carts. Ideally, we needed a fine dry day, with the river flood being low so that the water rose gradually, forming a pool behind the makeshift barrier. It was important that the dam should have a wide foundation so that the rising water did not wash everything away.

For us youngsters the most important feature was the food, with every farm sending along a basketful, each packed with meat sandwiches, buttermilk and cold tea. I remember one year when the children forgot to guard the baskets. How the dogs enjoyed that feast!

Once the dam wall was strong enough and of sufficient height to block the river, the flow below the dam would have been reduced to a trickle. It meant a good harvest of trout left stranded in the shallows. We knew that it would only be a matter of time before the damn was full, pouring water over the wall and offering the fish salvation once more.

When the work on the dam was finished, each farm would bring their flocks over in turn, their order based on the various farms' shearing day. And, as we would be the first on the calendar, our sheep would be the first to be washed. As noted, our shearing day was on the last day in June. Should there be an extra Friday in the month, that would be Dolgoch's turn. Should the last day be a Thursday, the date would be advanced a whole week, meaning an early shearing that year.

On the morning of the washing Father would ride, with his dogs following, to meet his neighbouring farmers. Together they would gather their flocks on the mountain, while I would be carried in Alf's cart. I would pester Alf, begging to be allowed to drive. My pleadings would eventually melt his heart and I would be allowed to drive the horse and cart – but only on the level stretches of the road.

I never discovered why the food in the baskets was always far tastier than the food I ate at home. And how I would long to hear Father bringing work to a halt with a shout of,

'Right lads, let's have a little something to eat!'

On the way home all of our men would travel back in the cart, meaning that Alf dare not let me drive. The return journey would be a riotous affair, with everyone in high spirits. My mind, however, would be on the fish frying in the pan, making me feel as hungry as a horse. I felt like a cowboy on the range in his covered wagon as I watched the offside wheel flirting with the edge of the road high above the precipice. There were no signs of any Indians!

I knew come sheep washing day that our shearing day was only a week or so away. And what a week that would be, with everyone pitching in to ensure that everything would be ready by the big day. Uncle Danny and his son Rol, who were local carpenters, would tidy up the house, including papering and painting. Doors would need hanging, broken windows would need panes of glass replaced. Wooden benches would need repairs. Father would be out, armed with a scythe and sickle attacking any nettles he could see around the farmyard. Alf, Jack and I would scrub the cowshed and the wash house. Then we would mix lime with water and use the resulting whitewash to brighten some of the buildings, especially the back wall of the house after removing any errant weeds that had invaded the cracks.

In the house all the dinner plates, dishes, jugs and cutlery would be taken out of the two-piece cupboard and washed, dried and laid out on the parlour table. Goose wings, remnants of the Christmas cull, that had been encased in pages of the *Cambrian News* would be unwrapped and waved around as Mam and the maid dusted every nook and cranny. The ornamental brass horse decorations would be taken down and polished by Grandma with dusters made out of torn shirts and vests, the smell of Brasso pervading everywhere.

Entering the house during those last few days prior to shearing was like walking through a minefield. And the warnings issued from every direction,

'Don't walk over the clean tiles! Watch where you put your feet! Mind that wet paint!'

Meat would be made ready. The beef came from Llew the Butcher's shop in Tregaron, while the mutton would be from one of our own fattened wethers. The unfortunate ewe would be chosen by Mam from a line-up of sheep in the cowshed. It was exactly like diners in some restaurants today being allowed to choose their fish from a tank. The condemned creature would be slaughtered and I would then hang the ewe ready for cutting.

The next chore would be chopping firewood for the wall oven. It would be used non-stop for days what with baking bread, slabs of cakes and rice puddings. Mam's rice puddings were legend. She would be proud of the fact that, after serving her offerings, not one spoonful would be left over. Somehow, amidst all the pandemonium, Mam would, one way or another, find time to have her hair permed. This would be carried out at home at ten o'clock on the eve of shearing day.

On Friday morning, with all the men having left for Dolgoch's shearing, peace and quiet would pervade the house. Mam would sit at the kitchen table sipping tea and looking as if she had been to hell and back.

For the coming month the men would be away every day either washing sheep, gathering them or shearing them. Mam would take the opportunity of visiting the homes of those women that had helped us. I learnt to shear when I was very young, as it was a good excuse for missing school and also showed other children that I had graduated from distributing thin lengths of muslin for tying the legs of sheep or from merely carrying sheep to the shearers.

I have often wondered who decides in which times children are born. All I know is that today's children have far less work to do that I did during my childhood. For example, fire was needed for practically everything, meaning that there was a need for firewood and coal. It was my job to fetch and carry. The sheep were marked with pitch that came in blocks, meaning that they would have to be heated over a fire. The branding iron would need to be red-hot from the fire. Every female sheep had to be additionally burn marked with the iron across the top of the nose. Our mark was 'A' or 'T', the first denoting 'Arch' and the second being the first letter of Father's Christian name, Thomas or Tommy. The nose burn was in the form of the letter 'N', denoting the first letter of Nachlog, the colloquial name for the farm.

I was taught to shear at twelve years old at Nantstalwyn's shearing, a farm high on Tregaron mountain that owned some three thousand sheep. Back then they kept wethers. I began in the fold with a tramp known as Carnera. He caught the sheep and I the lambs. He always wore a mask over his face and sucked on a piece of twig. He would never talk to me. At dinnertime one of the girls would bring his food out to him. He would empty the pudding over his dinner and eat the lot together! After dinner and before resuming the shearing, many of the men would play card games such as Pontoon, and Carnera would then join in. And invariably he would win the largest kitty. Catching sheep for the shearer with Carnera was no easy task, especially when I helped him catch the wethers. Rod Williams would urge me,

'Let the bugger catch them himself!'

Next to Rod would be Dai Cornwal, who always brought with him two pairs of shears. He was once asked by Joe Bryneithinog why he needed two. Dai's answer was,

'When one becomes overheated I can turn to the other!'

That day I borrowed one of Dai's shears and tried my hand at shearing. I never looked back. After that I never had to catch sheep again.

There would be a shearing in the neighbourhood every day except Sunday for a whole month. Every farm had its appointed date and it would be adhered to religiously as if it were set in stone. Any farm failing to shear because of inclement weather would be sent to the back of the queue. The sheep would be sent back to the mountain and the shearing day held at the end of the season. It is worth noting the shearing calendar in our neighbourhood.

The last Monday in June	Nantyrhwch
Tuesday	Penwernhir
Wednesday	Maesglas

Thursday	Great Abbey
Friday	Dolgoch
Saturday	Dolebolion and Dolbeudiau
Monday	Nantstalwyn
Tuesday	Berthgoed
Wednesday	Cefngaer and Blaenglasffrwd
Thursday	Maesllyn and Llwyngronwen
Friday	Nantymaen
Saturday	Bryneithinog and Troedrhiw
Monday	Frongoch
Tuesday	Grofftau
Wednesday	Pantyfedwen and Bronhelem
Thursday	Tŷ'n Ddôl and Gilfach y Dwn Fawr
Friday	Wernfelen
Saturday	Allt Ddu and Caemadog
Monday	Nantllwyd and Brynhope
Tuesday	Bronmwyn
Wednesday	Gilfach y Dwn Fach and Gwndwn Gwinau
Thursday	Hafodnewydd
Friday	Tywi Fechan
Saturday	Bwlch y Ddwyallt

Those attending would travel there on horseback and all the horses would be kept for that day in a nearby field used as a paddock. At Nantstalwyn's shearing there would be around a hundred ponies present. Other shearers and helpers would be taken in two lorries, one supplied by T.L. Hughes from Pontrhydfendigaid and the other by J.D. James, Tregaron. At the larger shearings on the mountains a count of the stock would be recorded on a small, square piece of wood. This would be done by using a pocket knife to cut a notch across the block, with one notch equalling ten sheep. One side would record breeding sheep, another the wethers, the third would denote the number of sheep to be sold, and the fourth the rams. The details would be called out to the teller by whoever was in charge of the marking carried out with pitch. This activity would be set aside for one of the old heads, as it was regarded as a very responsible task. A bench would always be placed beside the shearing shed, reserved for the old and the experienced. They would often wear straw hats and long yellow smocks. There they would pass judgement on the shearing standards, the quality of the lambs, and other important aspects.

Following all the excitement of the shearing season, I would always find it difficult to settle down to life back on the farm, before turning then in earnest to the hay harvest.

8

The Order of the Boot

IF 1947 WAS memorable, the following year was even more pivotal. September arrived far too soon meaning that the dreaded move to Tregaron Grammar School was imminent. It meant walking the mile to the village to catch the school bus. Mam had put together for me the statutory school uniform. With five children to care for, she couldn't afford to buy everything.

First I needed shoes. Mam took me to Thomas Evans' shoemaker's shop in Ffair Rhos. But, rather than sell me shoes, Thomas insisted on making me a pair of heavy boots.

'I'll make you a pair that the King of England would be proud to wear,' said Thomas. 'That is, if he was man enough to carry them.'

The boots arrived and I realised the significance of his promise. They were heavy hobnailed boots more suitable for mountain climbing than for school. I was given Aunty Mat's old school tie, one of Uncle Will's old shirts that was two sizes too big for me, and a coat and trousers from Miss Rees that had once graced her sister's boy. I could well have been mistaken for a refugee. My only new clothes were my vest and underpants.

The first day dawned and I walked the mile to the Post

Office in the village square to catch Will Lloyd's red-and-white utility bus. The bus arrived and I made straight for the back seat. My welcome included a slap around the ear and a kick in the backside.

'Go to the front where you belong,' was the uncompromising message.

No one had bothered telling me that the back seat belonged exclusively to the seniors. We duly arrived, my left ear and my backside still smarting. The first hour and three-quarters thankfully passed without incident. I was given a glass of milk and out I went to the boys' playground behind the building. I hadn't even started looking around when a gang of seniors herded all of us newcomers into a nearby shed. We were ordered by a huge brute of a senior to either sing, recite or tell a joke. One by one we stepped forward, and I realised the object of it all. The seniors stuck a pin in our backsides. My turn arrived and I felt the pin. It felt more like a bayonet. Then I remembered my secret weapons – Thomas the Shoemaker's pair of clodhoppers. I kicked out, dropping my tormentors like ninepins. By the time I managed to make my escape, I was bloodied and minus my Aunty Mat's tie and Uncle Will's shirt buttons. Some of the seniors looked even worse.

I felt like running the six miles home, but then two or three of my new companions helped clean me up. My first day at school eventually passed and I had survived. The following morning the captain of 'Ship Ahoy' approached me. He was a fourth-former and he recruited me. Every Ship Ahoy team needed a minor pupil.

Ship Ahoy teams were made up of seven members, six big boys and one small. The team would stand by the shed, with the smallest member crouching and pressing his hands against the wall. Then another would crouch and hold on to the one in front of him. And so it went on until all seven were crouching in a line. Then, the leading boy in the line, me in our case, would jump forward making room for the next. This was repeated. Then all seven would jump on the backs of the opposing members attempting to dislodge them. The one who finished on top would win. Why it was called Ship Ahoy I am still none the wiser. However, from that day on I did not encounter any problems with the seniors, thanks to my ability in Ship Ahoy and Thomas the Shoemaker's hobnailed boots.

I had little interest in most of the subjects taught and I would have ignored them all had it not been for Miss Rees' enthusiasm. I wasn't able to get along at all with the English teacher, Dai Williams. His advice to me from the beginning was to forget any hopes of doing well academically, but rather to go to the Co-op to buy myself a pick and shovel. I got the impression that he detested farm children. To him we were just a nuisance. But Shanco Nantllwyd got the better of him one morning. Dai Williams asked to see his homework book. Shanco, as usual, said he had forgotten it. Dai Williams told him,

'Shanco Jones, the day you remember to bring in your homework book, I will drop down dead!'

Shanco replied like a shot, 'I'll bring it in first thing tomorrow morning, sir!'

As a farmer's son I saw little sense in learning Latin, especially as it was the last lesson on Friday afternoon with two days of freedom ahead of me. And things got from bad to worse between me and the Physics teacher, Mr Pardoe.

Thanks to him I believe I still hold the record time for writing a hundred lines as punishment dished out by him. Ted Wff and I spent one whole morning plotting to blow up both him and the laboratory with a bomb. Unfortunately neither Ted nor I were budding Barnes Wallises and the sadist Pardoe survived.

Most of my teachers, however, were excellent; among them Miss Boden, Miss Treharne, James Chemistry and Miss Williams History. I look back at them thankfully, not so much for educating me but rather for preparing me for the future. Even so, it was difficult for a farmer's son to appreciate homework and some of the strange subjects taught. That's when I remembered words spoken by John Jenkins, the village sage,

'If you ever find yourself sinking in mud, don't let it go over your boots. Look, rather, for a more solid path.'

And that's what I did. At Tregaron Grammar School at that time the curriculum included agricultural studies or Rural Science. It included practical work on a patch of land referred to as The Plot where vegetables were grown. They would all end up in the school canteen where the head cook, Mrs Williams, and her staff fed us. By the end of the year, thanks to John Jenkins' advice, I ended up being named as the most industrious agricultural pupil. This led to the teacher, Mr Griffiths, putting me and John Penbont, another farmer's son, in charge of The Plot. I should explain that being in charge meant sharing out the garden tools, cleaning them afterwards and then returning them to the shed. On the other hand, we did oversee the task of spreading manure along the furrows. And our greatest pleasure was to watch the others having to use their hands to spread it. They smelt worse than the inside of a pigsty afterwards.

It was through our cooperation with Mr Griffiths that we won our promotion. We would trundle a wheelbarrow full of potatoes over to the canteen. There, Mrs Williams would treat us to pudding leftovers. One day there were newly-baked jam tarts on the table and, foolishly, I ate one not realising that the jam was still hot. I burnt my mouth so badly that I couldn't eat properly for a week.

Mr Griffiths must have been pleased with us. After a few days overseeing the work on The Plot, we were invited to prune apple trees in his and Mrs Griffiths' garden. For a while he watched us from behind the kitchen door, but soon realised that we were competent and left. The following week we were sent to tidy Dr Davies' garden next door. Things were looking good. At this rate we would be excused lessons and could concentrate totally on gardening. And, to cap it all, the following week Mr Griffiths led us into the headmaster's garden right next door to the school. In D. Lloyd Jenkins' garden there were four apple trees, and half a dozen hens and a cockerel scratching around them.

Mrs Jenkins' clothesline ran across the garden and on this particular afternoon her fur coat was hanging on it being aired. John placed the ladder against the first apple tree and we began pruning. Like the Council's roadmen, we did not rush but rather took our time so that we could prolong the task as long as we could. Suddenly, the Rhode Island Red cockerel left its scratching and hobby of chasing hens and flew – landing on Mrs Jenkins' fur coat. John and I, instead of shooing it away, stood watching as the vulgar bird did what all cockerels have to do occasionally. He left his calling card on the coat.

We called Mrs Jenkins and out she rushed. She thanked us for alerting her. But when Mr Griffiths arrived and saw what had happened, he correctly summed up the situation and realised that we were guilty of a dereliction of duty. It took us a while to regain his faith in us. We realised that it would have been better for us and for the coat had we acted sooner. And especially for the cockerel, as it ended up the following Sunday on Mr and Mrs Jenkins' dinner table.

I began to realise that nature was a fickle companion. It could land someone in the muck up to the fifth bootlace. One afternoon I got off Will Lloyd's bus on the Square as usual only to confront Father's Saddleback sow coming to meet me. It was a huge black creature with a white band across its back. It was this characteristic, according to Alf, our farmhand, that gave the breed its name. Before I could even reach the errant creature, Davies the Policeman, who lived across the road, confronted me. He had only arrived in the village the previous week. He glared at me and enquired officiously,

'Is that your father's sow?'

I answered in the affirmative.

'Well,' he said, 'you'd better warn him that if he doesn't fetch it immediately I'll be serving him with a summons!'

'Father can't do too much about it,' I tried to explain. 'The sow is looking for a boar.'

Davies grabbed me by the scruff of the neck and lifted me bodily. Had Dafydd Hughes the Mason not been standing there I'm sure I would have received the full force of Davies' size twelve boot up my nether region. What did a policeman, a new one at that, know about the sexual life of a sow? The old girl, every time she felt the urge, would walk over to the Thomas family's place at Y Bryn to slake her passion before finding her own way back.

Many were the farmers who felt the lash of Davies' tongue should any of their animals stray onto the road. Dolfawr's bull would often find a gap in the hedge and wander onto the Dolau road. It only had to show its snout over the fence for Davies to be over there threatening a summons. This happened so often that Aeronian, the youngest brother, would always refer to him as Dolfawr's Cowman.

Davies and I, over the years, conducted our own personal little war. Perhaps I would be riding my bicycle at night without any lights. He would hide somewhere along the abbey road hoping to surprise me. Gradually I got to know his hiding places. One night, however, he found a new hidey-hole in Dolgoed's rhododendron bushes. As I pedalled past he grabbed me by the back of my coat. I somehow managed to divest myself of it. I cycled away leaving Davies holding my empty coat. He tried to trick me for months afterwards, inviting me nicely to call in at the police station to claim it. But I always denied it was mine.

I can freely confess today of having ridden my bike over the years without any semblance of a light, front or rear. Although I was never caught and taken to court and fined, I paid for it in other ways. I hit unseen obstacles more than once on dark nights. One night, I collided with a black cow that was lying in the middle of the road. I couldn't tell who was more frightened, me or the cow!

Davies' term as village policeman eventually came to an end. On his last day I called at the police station to claim my long-lost coat.

'I knew it was yours all along, you little devil!' said Davies.

But this time he smiled!

To reiterate, 1947 and 1948 were memorable for different reasons. But 1948 was memorable too for another reason. In February that year Father caught pneumonia. Until then I had never seen him in bed during daylight hours. Dr Davies from Tregaron and Nurse Davies from the village called regularly to press a hot poultice over his chest. Mam would constantly remind us of the need to keep away from upstairs. And I overheard Alf telling Tommy the Post that Father was as weak as a kitten.

Around this time we were inundated with a plague of rats. Some even found their way into the house. They overran the outbuildings, destroying the corn and gnawing at the swedes and mangolds and even dislodging stones from the walls. One day, as Mam went upstairs to tend to Father, she was met by over a dozen rats. The tray she was carrying flew up in the air. She screamed and ran back downstairs.

Animal feeds were decimated by the rats, and all the cats, as well as two dogs, fled. One night, my sister Glenys was heard crying in her bed. A rat had bitten her thumb and she had to receive treatment. We were all nervous wrecks.

Then, one afternoon, Alf returned from the village with a strange tale to tell. He had seen hundreds of rats led by a white rat crossing Cae Gwair and over the river towards

Dolebolion. What happened to us happened there – until they eventually disappeared from there as well.

All our animal feed had to be burnt as it had all been contaminated by rat droppings and had become poisonous. All the cats returned as well as one of the dogs. It brought to an end too a game that my school friend Charles Cornwal and I had been enjoying. We would creep quietly to the rickyard and look out for rat tails sticking out from holes in the wall. We would suddenly grab the tails and then smash the rats' heads against the wall. We were constantly warned by Alf that we could catch a nasty disease. As usual we ignored all his warnings.

With the disappearance of the rats things changed, but only slowly. Father recovered, but only gradually. He couldn't take on all the tasks he would undertake previously. I realised I was busier that before and was increasingly forgoing my homework. Farm work was getting interesting, with Father and Alf trusting me increasingly with chores that had been prohibited previously. Neglecting my studies didn't please Miss Rees or Mam. To them, I was college material. To Aunty Jenny Penddolfawr, I was destined for the cloth. One day I mentioned this to Alf who responded,

'Don't be such a bloody fool! There's no money in preaching!'

Miss Rees, Mam and Aunty Jenny's dreams faded away, especially after the autumn term that year. In November 1948 my mentor, Miss Rees, died. She was only fifty-seven. A few days later there were fourteen of us standing at her graveside, the dozen children that still attended the Abbey School and Marina Tŷ'n Cwm and myself who had just left for Tregaron Grammar School. Rain was whipping from across the river and running down the faces of the tombstones just as if God himself was crying and ruing his decision to reclaim her. We stepped forward to gaze down at her coffin, all fourteen of us. And that was when I became aware of her Christian name for the very first time. Engraved on the brass plate was:

Mary Gwendoline Rees C.M.

To someone who had never referred to her other than as Miss Rees, it was a strange realisation. The vicar in his tribute referred to her many talents. And I remembered the concerts and eisteddfods and dramas she had taught me to perform in. I recalled reciting at Glanrafon, a branch of the local Methodist chapel, built on the common. And I remembered Alf taking me there over Waunwen hill across to the common past Gilfach y Dwn Fach, the night as black as sin. Then, walking back after midnight and hearing footsteps following us across the field, we ran until we reached the gate only to realise that we had been running away from Gilfach y Dwn Fach's bullocks. Alf would also take me across Bronberllan fields to compete at Caersalem, the Baptists' meeting place in Ffair Rhos. And, of course, to every eisteddfod in the village.

Back then there were three drama groups in the neighbourhood, with Miss Rees in charge of two of them. She would always remind us of her credo,

'Make sure you respond to every situation that may arise.'

I remember in one play reaching for a teapot to pass around and the lid falling off and rolling away. Rather than carrying on and ignoring it, I picked up the lid and replaced it. She enjoyed that. Dai Hughes, however, was not impressed. He thought that I should have stayed in my chair.

A year later Dai was on stage in a play and wearing a false beard. During the interval between two acts he removed it. When he reappeared he was minus his beard. He had forgotten to replace it. As he appeared minus his beard, John Jenkins, who was playing one of the roles, realised what had happened and improvised with,

'I see that you have shaved since last we met, my friend.'

Dai rubbed his chin and, realising his gaffe, uttered a line that wasn't in the script,

'Damn! I've forgotten my beard!'

And off he went to the anteroom to retrieve his beard. He was to remember that exit for some time!

Had it not been for Miss Rees I would have had fewer interests in my life and would not have been able to contribute as much as I was able to give to the community. And who knows, had Miss Rees been allowed to live an extra decade, I would indeed have ended up in college and on my way to a totally different life. But, following her death, the call of the land grew ever stronger and more persuasive.

I spent a further three years at Tregaron Grammar School. Other than obeying the three or four teachers that I genuinely admired, I mostly caused havoc and was spending much of my time in the headmaster's room. During my last year, the last lesson on a Friday afternoon was difficult for two reasons. For one thing, I would be itching to get on the bus. As for the other, it was a music lesson. I hated music and it would be an ongoing war between Ted Morgan, the peripatetic music teacher, and us, tuneless farmers' sons.

I remember being in a music exam and sitting behind a

girl called Mari from Ystrad Meurig, the very same Mari who later became mad enough to marry me. She was always top in music and I could plainly see her exam paper from where I sat. A fortnight later I was called out in front of the others and lauded as the most improved music pupil in the class, earning seventy-five marks out of a possible one hundred. What a disappointment it was for Ted Morgan the following term to find me back at the bottom with just five marks. It was Mari's fault for moving to sit at the front!

Almost before I even realised it, I was exiting Will Lloyd's school bus on the village square for the last time. And the tie, the grey pair of trousers, the cap and the bag were consigned to the dustbin of history. I was now ready to be a proper farmer.

9

The Farming Year

BEFORE MOVING ON to life after my initiation as a full-time farmer, perhaps it would be worth looking closer at the various farming activities over the year, month by month, especially around the time when it all really began for me. Looking back I believe I was fortunate to be born in the neighbourhood at a time when it remained relatively old-fashioned. This was especially true in my family's case. Father was the last farmer in these parts to buy a tractor. He remained true to horsepower until his latter days. I certainly witnessed the great watershed that now seems so long ago, so far away that I sometimes query the accuracy of the date on my birth certificate.

The order remained unchanged for years. On the annual calendar New Year's Day was not only the first, but also the most important day of the year by far for a farmer's boy. As it turned midnight I would be woken up – not that I needed prompting – and Alf would be waiting to accompany me on my annual round to gather *calennig*. This meant calling at farmsteads around the neighbourhood, wishing householders a Happy New Year. These tidings would be acknowledged by the head of the household, with some money being thrown from an upstairs window, hopefully silver rather than coppers.

My round would begin at Dolgoed, then on to Dolteifi and as far as Troedrhiw Dolau along the road to the village. Then I would cross the river to Dolebolion and follow the valley to Caemadog before reaching Penddolfawr where Aunty Jenny would have breakfast waiting.

At these neighbourhood farms, where many of the farmers were either relatives or close friends, I would receive as much as a pound on condition that I was the first to call. There was also an old custom, still prevalent back then, that the first person to call should be male. This would please the ladies of the house in particular.

After breakfast I would walk across Bronberllan heath as far as Tŷ'n Fron in Ffair Rhos, my grandmother's home and where Uncle Jenkin and Aunty Mat lived also. All three would dig deep. Uncle Jenkin, however, wouldn't part with his offering until I had recited a poem. Despite Grandmother's pleading to hand over the money and allow me to go on my way, he would stand firm. It was a case of no poem, no money! But I wouldn't grumble. New Year's Day was a busy but a very profitable day for me.

January on the farm meant endless log cutting. Kindling would be needed for the big kitchen, the parlour and the wash house. The wall oven in the kitchen would need to be filled with logs at least once a week for baking loaves and slabs of cake. The fire beneath the mantle chimney, where there would always be a boiling cauldron full of potatoes and food leftovers, had to be tended. Every time the cauldron came to the boil it was lifted on a fireside crane and swung out and placed on the stone floor. There, some oats would be stirred into the contents. This was fodder for the pigs.

It should be remembered that logs would be cut with

nothing more sophisticated that an axe and a cross-saw. During January the men would be forever dragging logs to be cut, some from the riverbeds, others which had been blown down by the winter winds. Often there would be sizeable branches left over after hedging. Hedging was important for keeping boundaries secure, as there was no pig fencing or sheep fencing back then. Gaps in hedges would often be filled with cut blackthorn branches to stop sheep from wandering and devouring vegetables in village gardens. Still, some of these woollen Houdinis managed to escape, meaning that Alf or Jack, the farmhands, would have to fetch them back. Father would never join them.

One Saturday I discovered why. Alf and I had been called to a back garden in Teifi Street where two of our rams were attacking the cabbage patch. I went in to try and shoo them away when, from the loft above, came an unexpected shower. No, not rain, but the contents of a chamber pot aimed accurately from an overhanging bedroom window. From then on I would never enter a garden without first sending in the dogs. And I learnt to look up before passing beneath any bedroom window!

An important day in January was pig slaughtering day. There would be three such days during the year, the first in January, the second in February and the third in October. My Uncle John Morgan would come over from Gilfach y Dwn Fawr to act as chief executioner. He would arrive in time for dinner and then, without further ado, he would get down to work. While I was at school I managed to escape from witnessing the bloody ritual every time. It was a different matter after I left.

The pig would be dragged to the wash house, a rope

between its teeth and tied around its upper snout. Alf would always do the leading, while Father grabbed the creature's tail to guide it. John Morgan knelt as if in supplication in front of the pig before plunging in the knife.

Following the slaughter, the creature's body would be stretched out on a bench. Boiling hot water was poured over it to facilitate the task of shaving off its bristles. Then came the disembowelling and the cutting. We children would eagerly wait the removal of the bladder. This would be inflated using a bicycle pump, the end tied and then used as a ball. Inevitably the bladder would soon burst, bringing the game to a premature and abrupt end.

We children played our part in cutting up slabs of salt for rubbing into the pig's flesh so that it would remain fresh. Mam would buy the salt in large blocks, what we referred to as *cerrig halen* in Welsh. She had a special device to grind the slabs into powder.

Following the pig's demise there would be a full week of devouring fresh meat, with bits of spareribs distributed among friends and neighbours. Tommy the Postman would be invited to sit with us at the table.

A few years later, Uncle John Morgan began rolling the sides of meat, which is turning the sides of meat to form rolls, thus ensuring that the bacon would be streaky. It wasn't an easy task so I would sometimes accompany him around the surrounding farms to help him out. Rolling the side meant a better mix of red and white meat. Not one piece of the pig would be wasted. Mam would make brawn out of the pig's head; she would also boil the trotters, and the cheeks would be stuffed.

I have heard some farmers' claim that January was always

the easiest month of the year as there was little to do on the land. But, as well as chopping logs and slaughtering the pig, there was chaffing to do, as well as pulping and feeding the animals regularly. On dry days we would take out manure for spreading, using two carts. The cow dung had been so compacted in the sheds by the cows' trampling that it would have to be offloaded using cramps. It would be left in heaps on the field; with seven yards between each heap. It would then be spread using pitchforks. This was tedious work, especially to someone working alone. Often, on frosty days, the men would take the opportunity of crossing the frozen river with loads of manure to be spread on Pwllbwdan field. The ice would be thick enough to bear the weight of the horse and cart. It would be difficult to imagine such hard frost nowadays.

February would arrive; time to bring out the working horses for the opening of the ploughing season. Father would keep six shire horses and two cob mares indoors over the winter. Sometimes two colts would also share the loosebox. It was important to take advantage of every dry day as there would be four large fields to plough. There would be one for oats, another for wheat, and a third would have black oats taking up one half and mixed corn the other. In the fourth we would plant potatoes and grow swedes and mangolds.

For the fallow land Father would use the one-furrowed plough, but for the stubble he would often use the two-furrowed plough. Around the end of the first week in February the threshing machine would arrive, towed by Rhys Waunwen and accompanied by Dan Bronant. They would arrive mid afternoon, set up the thresher and carry out any running repairs that were needed. Then, following a meal, they would leave for home on their Bantam motorbikes. I remember seeing the Bantam symbol on the petrol tank. I would pester Rhys, begging to be allowed to ride his bike. He would always refuse.

'You want to ride this?' he would exclaim. 'This would fly you over the house before you could even spit!'

I would get up early the following day to help neighbour Dai Cornwal erect a wire fence around the ricks to keep the rats from escaping and allow the dogs to catch them. Dai would always bring his terrier with him, but would not let him join the other dogs inside the fence despite the fact that he would boast that his terrier was the best ratter in the county. I remember Mam having a marmalade-coloured cat that had just had kittens when Dai called with his terrier in tow. Before the terrier could blink, the cat planted its claws in its back. Suddenly, the terrier was a greyhound as it disappeared down the road.

By the end of threshing day there would be a tall, wide straw rick in the barn ready for chaffing, a heap of chaff for the store cattle, and the seeds safely stored in the cart house loft.

February meant slaughtering another pig and the last opportunity until autumn for a pig's bladder to play with. Immediately following the pig's demise, the cover would be removed from the store of seed potatoes. Two women from the village, Sal, Dai Cornwal's wife, and her friend Averina Hughes, would spend a day choosing and picking out suitable potatoes for different purposes. Seed potatoes and potatoes for eating were segregated and bagged, while the rest would be taken by Jack Sais in a wheelbarrow to feed to the cows. Father favoured Kerr's Pink and King Edward potatoes.

Thomas Arch, the first member of our family to occupy Abbey Farm

My great-grandmother, with my father and his sister Mary Anne

With my parents, aged three

With Beti, my eldest sister

Four of the five children: Beti, Dai, Glenys and me

My father with his favourite bay pony

My father on the famous Billy Boy

Myself on the 'gambo', with the grey mare Flower

My brother Dai and I on the hills above Strata Florida

Sheep-dipping day on the mountain

The old water wheel that powered the barn machinery

The famous Buck print of the abbey, with the farmhouse in the background

Among the fifth-form pupils at Tregaron Grammar School

With one of many successful Ystrad Fflur Young Farmers' Club drama casts

With the winning cast of the play *Rusalka*

At one of our YFC's annual dinners

Cast of the all-Wales YFC mime competition at the Kings Hall, Aberystwyth

With one of our YFC's winning public speaking competition

At one of the national YFC county organisers' meetings in Harlech

Our winning team at the inaugural all-Wales book reading competition

Being presented following my seventh year as Montgomeryshire YFC Organiser

Producer, with the winning all-Wales drama competition – Montgomeryshire

An aerial view of Strata Florida from the hill above

Up among the hills gathering the Abbey Farm flocks

The mountain sheep beginning their trek down the valley

The sheep arriving at the farm from their mountain grazing

The gargantuan pilgrim statue, sculpted by Glenn Morris, on the hill above the farm

Meeting The Prince of Wales, with brother Dai and his son Iwan

© David Austin

The spreading beech tree almost hiding Strata Florida church

The ancient yew tree above the grave of Dafydd ap Gwilym

The stained glass altar window at Strata Florida church

The teacher's desk from the Abbey School, and a picture of my great-grandmother now in the farmhouse

With members
of the family in
the *Cegin Fawr*
(Big Kitchen)

Daughter
Mererid
leaving the old
farmhouse for
her wedding

Family
members,
together with
Professor David
Austin and his
wife Gaenor,
outside the old
farmhouse

My wife Mari and I
with the present Arch
farming family
© Strata Florida Trust

The Arches
under the arch!
© Strata Florida Trust

With Mari, under the great
arch
© Strata Florida Trust

The Arch family outside a Lincolnshire church where some of our ancestors lie

The Arch family on holiday

Another awayday for the family

In the commentator's box at the Royal Welsh Show

Enjoying the sunshine ringside at the show

By the third week of the month the cows would begin to calve. The first would be Cochen. This meant the onset of the dreaded churning of the milk and, just as bad, the separating that followed. By the end of the month lambing would inevitably begin, and we would look out excitedly for the first-born lamb of the year. Before 1947 the custom was to start lambing at the beginning of March. But, following those terrible losses, it was pushed forward a month.

The first day of March would be almost as important to us children as the first of January and all of us would search for daffodils to wear. Those that failed would be mocked mercilessly. What with the lambing, the continuing work on the land and feeding the stock, the men had very little opportunity to help Mam. As a result, I would be called upon more and more to give her a helping hand.

Every Friday afternoon after tea I would help Mam carry butter and eggs to Dick Rees' shop and then help her bring home the groceries. Practically every farming family had an arrangement that would mean a system of bartering. They would run up a debt for goods bought, including animal foodstuff, and pay it off once a year, usually at the end of October. Against that the shopkeeper would deduct what he owed for the butter and eggs.

Another of my duties would be to cycle over to Strata Florida railway station, two miles away, to collect boxes of day-old chicks, hens and turkeys that would have arrived on the train. I could always guarantee that, by the time I had returned home with the boxes, one or two of the chicks would have died. Ensuring that the others would survive their first few days would mean constant care. Turkey chicks especially were delicate, and would be suffering with some disease or other constantly. Often I would hold the chicks in turn while Mam, with what looked like a small pair of bellows, would blow a whitish powder up their nostrils as a precaution against a disease called Gapeworm infection. I must have inhaled as much of the powder as the birds did.

The first piglets of the year would also arrive in March. And when a sow would settle in for the night, I would be sent to the pigsty to make sure she didn't lie on one of her litter. I would sometimes spend an hour or two there while the men were milking and feeding the cows. A Saddleback sow could be a nasty creature, baring its crocodile-like teeth. I would tend to all these chores as well as feeding any orphaned lambs.

The end of the month would see us sowing corn and planting potatoes, and I would sometimes miss school to help out. The sowing would be done by hand. Mam would prepare a sling made of white canvas that would hang from the shoulder and be tied at the back. This would be full of the seeds that Father would cast as he walked. As he reached the headland, Alf would be there to refill the canvas with fresh seed. Having covered the tilled ground with seed, Alf would then do the harrowing ensuring that the seeds were covered with soil. Soon rows of green shoots would appear, running in straight lines along the tracks of Father's furrows.

Potato planting would mean bringing in some of the village women to lend a hand. They would plant the potatoes, the men having already laid cow dung along the furrows. Then Father would close the furrows with the moulder. In return for their labour the women were allocated a row of potatoes each, enough to see them through the winter. The corresponding furrows would be identified with pegs, as was the type of potato planted. Dai Cornwal demanded to mark his furrow at both ends as he believed his species of potato to be special. His identification marks also served as a warning for others to keep off. Should Dai have a dozen or so seedling potatoes to spare, he would give them to me to plant.

April always began with us children up to all sorts of mischief on April Fool's Day. I remember fooling Alf once by running to him crying, telling him that a piglet had suffocated beneath the pigsty door. Alf ran over only for me to laugh at him. My acting lessons with Miss Rees were obviously having an influence! As for the pigs, how I hated cleaning out the pigsty every Saturday morning. No matter how thoroughly I scrubbed myself afterwards, I would still stink like a sewerage. Fortunately, by the end of April, the last of the piglets would be sold. Father would take them away in a cart covered with netting to stop them escaping. Every other householder would keep a pig in those days.

The last Saturday of the month was ear-marking day for our lambs. The outhouses would all be cleared of dung and the dungheap removed from the yard. The planted swedes and mangolds would be covered with most of the manure, the remainder kept for the rapeseed later on. Corn would be sown, although wet weather could mean postponing the barley until early May.

Father always kept a Shorthorn bull. It was a 'Society' bull, meaning that neighbouring farmers could use it to service their herd. During late April and early May, someone would bring over a cow almost daily. One day, when Father and Alf returned to stable the horses, they saw Twm Gargoed stranded on top of the dungheap having managed to escape from the bull that was pawing the ground and glaring at him. For once he had nothing to say, as he had brought his troubles upon himself by releasing the bull without permission. The bull was always suspicious of Twm after that but not half as suspicious as Twm was of the bull!

The men spent much of May harvesting peat. Here again neighbouring farmers joined together for the common cause. The peat would be cut forming a pit, and the turfs laid out at its ends and turned regularly to dry. Our peat source was six miles up the mountain and it would need three or four cartloads to fill the shed and keep us going over the winter.

Around this time we would also start moving the sheep flocks back up the mountain, lot by lot. A lot numbered some one hundred and fifty sheep. On the mountain they would not be enclosed, meaning that they were free to roam – some returning as far down as Pantcarnau gate which was only some three miles from home. And, during inclement weather, they would almost all make their way down there.

We would also take other flocks up there on behalf of their owners, charging so much per head for the service. These would remain there until October and tended to keep to their traditional patches without wandering too far, meaning that they would be fairly easy to locate for shearing day. Sheep owned by Tŷ'n Dolau, Bronant, for instance, would tend to graze at Olchfa; and Dolfawr's sheep at Llethr Gwared Bach. I remember Daniel James Dolfor once asking Father for permission to send his sheep up over the summer. Father initially refused, as he didn't have a shepherd at the time to deal with an extra flock and to get them used to their patch. He compromised however by selling him a flock of four year olds that were sent up the mountain in the autumn and returned in spring. It was a failure though, as they merged with other flocks making it almost impossible to gather them together when it became time to bring them down.

With the sheep flocks absent, attention would turn to the hay fields. Hedges and fences would be made more secure to keep the cows out of the hay fields. Alf and I would then fetch the drill for sowing smaller sized seeds kept in the storehouse loft. We would clean the drill thoroughly and oil all the moving parts. Father would then attach it to Flower, the shire horse, for sowing swedes and mangolds; he holding the drill steady and guiding it, while I led the horse. Father and I would squabble over the empty seed bags. He wanted them for storing the sand used to hone the scythe, while I wanted them for keeping my ferrets.

One chore that I never looked forward to was collecting all the lamps and cleaning them so that they would be ready for the next winter. On the plus side, the month of May meant the rivers running in full flood and the water turned brown. Then I would go out fishing with John Jenkins. In other words, poaching. John would say philosophically,

'If we don't catch anything, we won't be depriving anyone. If we do catch something, it will be a bonus.'

And catch something we would do every time.

June would be heralded with the clatter of hooves on the road as the stallion owner arrived. He would be met by mare owners from around the neighbourhood, there to service their mares. Cob stallions and shire stallions would arrive in turn. Tall stories would be shared. Jack Hughes would always address Father with the same words,

'Tommy, what in the world do you want with that big

clumsy workhorse when you could use a cob to do the same work for you?'

Father would tend to agree with him, but never changed his ways. Nothing but a workhorse would do for him for ploughing and other heavy work. Scuffling, that is clearing out the weeds and trash from between the rows and taking out the weaker plants to allow the rest to thrive, meant wearing sacks around legs as it involved a lot of kneeling. Dai Cornwal once commented,

'Tommy, I must be spending more time down on my knees than any minister of religion!'

I have already detailed the hustle and bustle of the shearing season, especially our own with all the preparations and shearing day itself. The weekend that followed our shearing would be sheer heaven. Immediately following Dolgoch's shearing the day after ours, Father would ride up to the woods on the grey pony or on the black cob to take a look at our dozen or so ponies that grazed there. He would bring them all down to the yard. He would then choose from among them three of the four year olds, cornering them and placing a halter over each one's head and then tie them in the stalls. Never having been haltered before and not used to being indoors, there would be much tugging and kicking from the ponies. After they quietened down somewhat, Father would place special bits in their mouths ready for attaching the bridles. Around midday on Saturday they would be led out to be ridden for the first time, meaning we would have three extra ponies to ride over the rest of the shearing season. By the end of the season they would be docile enough to carry children.

As he would be away shearing somewhere or other six

days a week, the only time Father could view the sheep on the mountain would be on a Sunday. And I would be taken with him up to the hills and get to know the mountain paths, those that were safe. He would warn me to keep well away from those that were dangerous for both rider and steed. Having reached the mountain he would lead me along the path that followed the Graig Wen fence. On we would ride to Esgair Warnen, heading towards the far corner where the path reached up to Foel Uchaf and to Moel Prysgau farm, then back to Llethr Gwaered and down towards the track that led to Tywi Fechan.

There, Father would always call to see Ifan Davies. Tywi Fechan was five miles up the mountain. He would always take with him a copy of the *Welsh Gazette*. Ifan was a big man, well over six feet tall and as broad as a barn door. Legend had it that he had never spent a single day suffering with any illness and, as a result, had never visited a doctor nor had a doctor visited him. It came as quite a surprise therefore, one Sunday in early July, to reach the house and be told by his wife, Marged Ann, that he had taken to his bed. He had been out shearing all week and had seemed fine. Father and I were taken upstairs to see him. I will never forget the sight of his swollen left hand. It seemed as big as a rugby ball and was a purplish colour. He was obviously in great pain but refused point-blank Father's offer of sending me to notify the doctor. Eventually he agreed to allow me to go to Tregaron to see the doctor before school the following day.

When the doctor duly arrived he realised immediately that Ifan was suffering with anthrax. Any normal person would have long died. And die Ifan eventually did two days later. His wife then caught it but luckily survived. Following an inspection of the animals it was discovered that one of the dogs was the carrier, although the dog itself seemed quite healthy. No one bothered to examine neither Father nor myself, although we had been in close contact with Ifan. Today we would have been kept in an isolation ward until cleared medically.

The week following Ifan's death I would be sent up to Tywi Fechan after school to milk the cows, three of them, and feed the calves. One evening, there I was milking away all on my own when someone walked in. It was Ifan! I spilled all the milk in the bucket and my hair stood on end. No one had told me that Ifan had a brother who was almost identical. In the gloom of the cowshed he looked exactly like his brother. I have never been so frightened in my life. No wonder that I later lost all my hair. I often look at Ifan Davies' tombstone. He died 12 July 1949 and was sixty-three years old.

The last week of the shearing season would mean it was time to turn to mowing the seeded hay laid earlier beneath the barley. It would always be lush grass peppered with a profusion of red clover. After the mowing it would, should rain arrive, be gathered in heaps or haycocks and left until dry weather. We would bring it in with help from some of the villagers, among them Dafydd Hughes and Hugh Jones, themselves smallholders. In return for their help, Father would let them borrow our horse and haycart to bring in their own hay.

The last Saturday of the month would be the Sunday school trip day. The popular destinations would be Rhyl or Llandudno, Porthcawl or Swansea. What with us children stuffing ourselves with toffee apples and candyfloss, the bus would have to stop here and there for some of us to be sick at the roadside. Jane Davies from Lisburne Row would always be there demanding a fish and chip stop on the way home. And so we would have an additional stop for Jane to be sick. She always laid the blame on whoever had fried the fish.

July and August overlapped naturally, with haymaking an important part of both. By the middle of August we would have finished with the hay fields and would have moved on to the sparser heaths. Should it be a warm summer, Father would mow and harvest large areas, but, should the summer be wet, the cows would be turned in to graze the peaty land.

As soon as the haymaking was over, Mam and Grandma Tŷ'n Fron would head for Llanwrtyd Wells for three days to take the waters and visit a few distant cousins who lived there. They would return with bottles full of the spa water, sipping from them occasionally. I remember Glenys and I taking a few sly sips and spitting it out. It tasted like what I would imagine cow pee tasting like.

I looked forward to another trip up the mountain for the sheep dipping at Tywi Fechan. I would travel in the cart with Mam and Alf, with the food that Mam and the maid had prepared. On one occasion Davies the Policeman arrived and demanded that every sheep be held in the dip for a full minute each. Ned, one of our neighbours, decided to do something about it. He threw some of the rams in so haphazardly that the dip splashed all over Davies. He didn't stay long after that.

Then would come the opportunity for another trip in the cart up the mountain to bring down the dried peat turfs. By now I had learnt my lesson, and kept a close watch on the dogs so that they didn't devour the sandwiches and the buttermilk brought up with us in the cart.

Mam was a fervent Baptist, and when the *Cyrddau Mawr* or the big religious meetings were held towards the end of the month, we all had to attend. We would attend the afternoon meeting and then it would be tea and cakes in the vestry before returning for the evening meeting. The chapel would be so packed that extra benches had to be brought in from the vestry. For weeks afterwards Mam would repeat some of the wisdoms of the visiting preachers, giants such as Jubilee Young. She could talk about them as eloquently as John David Hopkins the Shoemaker could talk about boxers Tommy Farr and Joe Louis.

August would end with the village agricultural show. With Father being such a keen horseman, our shires, cobs and ponies would be prepared and turned out looking their best. Father, with Alf and Jack, would spend the morning washing and grooming the horses' coats. Long plaits of grass and flowers would be interwoven with the shire horses' manes. The racehorses would be kept without any water before their competitions and the smell of liniment pervaded the stables. One year, and I much too young to take a horse to the show, Charles Cornwal and I groomed Wag, the sheepdog, and led her there in all her glory. In fact, she was awarded a red card in the dog show.

The next year I was allowed to take our Shorthorn cow, Brocen, to the show, aided by Jack. She didn't win but on our way home she jumped in the river dragging Jack and I with her. From then on I stuck to dogs and horses, and agreed with Jack Sais that a cow was only for milking or eating.

Before August ended it would mean a trip with Mam to Aberystwyth where she would buy new clothes for us for the coming new school year. So important was this event that

Dick Jones would fetch us in his taxi and take us as far as the Red Lion where the green Crosville bus would be waiting. The bus seemed to stop to pick up passengers in every hamlet and village, and by the time we reached Trawscoed I felt as sick as a dog. I would always try to sit near the door so I could gulp in the fresh air. That didn't stop my stomach from rising to my throat. At the top of Penparcau I had to get out and walk and meet Mam and the others beneath the Town Clock. By then I would have regained my appetite and we would all eat fish and chips in the nearby restaurant.

Should the weather have been kind in August, the men would waste no time at the beginning of September before opening swathes with their scythes around the perimeters of the corn fields to allow the binder to enter. This would be when Father would bring out the small sacks that had once held swede and mangold seeds but now contained grit. Fixed on the shaft of the scythe would be a sharpening tool, a long four-sided wooden implement with a handle. Father would take off the sharpening tool and cover it with fat. Then he would dip the wooden tool into a bagful of grit until it was thickly covered. He would then turn the scythe upside down, the blade on his shoulder with the point facing outwards. Then he would stroke the sharpening tool along the cutting edge. Soon the blade would be as sharp as a cut-throat razor. He would then start swinging and cutting, the loose corn tied in sheaves and left on one side until the binder had made one or two turns around the field. Then the binder would really get to work.

Three or four villagers would come over to lend a hand with the stacking, as well as trying to catch some of the rabbits attempting to escape the binder's cutters. Sometimes the binder's canvas would split, meaning that I had to cycle full pelt to John David Hopkins the Shoemaker for a skein of waxed thread. By my return the split canvas would have been removed so that Father could sow it back together. With any luck weather-wise, the corn could remain in stacks until it was brought in. But should we have wet weather the stacks would be brought together to build ricks. No one would dream of bringing in the sheaves until they had heard the church bell ringing three times, signifying that three Sundays had passed since the corn had been cut and was now ready to harvest. To a growing lad, whose ambition was to be a farmer, nothing could be better than missing two or three days of schooling to help load the flat cart and be allowed to ride home on top of the load with other schoolchildren jealously watching from the schoolyard or out through the classroom windows.

Following on from the corn harvest it would be time to fetch down the mountain sheep that were to be sold, as well as the ewes. These would be four year olds with a full set of teeth which would be bought to raise lambs on the lowlands for another three or four years. Having been selected, their coats would be trimmed and soil would be rubbed in their coats to give them colour. They would then be turned onto the stubble ground to await their sale.

Then there would be one more trip up the mountains to bring back the rest of the peat, before thatching the sheaves in the ricks. What with a dozen ricks in the yard, we would need loads of rushes and the flat cart would trundle back and forth carrying home loads of rushes scythed the previous day.

September would come to an end with the bullocks being turned into the aftergrass to prepare them for the end-of-year markets. Unlike today, they would all be Shorthorns, apart from a few crossed Herefords.

After thatching the ricks, we would turn our attention to cutting and harvesting bracken. No one would use straw bedding in those days. Straw would be used as fodder. I remember Alf and I cutting bracken on a rather steep bank above the road in the Glasffrwd valley. Having been scything all afternoon, we started rolling the bracken down the bank. Things went well until the growing bundle started rolling down the slope of its own volition. It landed on the road, just as Dick Jones drove past in a taxi carrying a load of schoolchildren. It took us a good half-hour to clear the road of the obstruction. Dick, to his credit, got out to help but the children ensured that everyone in the valley got to hear of our escapade.

By now the first of the three pigs would be fattening in the sty. To us schoolchildren October meant one thing – the potato holidays as they were referred to then. As in the case of the shearing, here again we would see the exchange of labour during the potato harvest. Most of the villagers by then would have exhausted their own rows, apart from Dai Cornwal who had his own ways of doing things. Picking potatoes could be a laborious task and very hard on the lower back with all the bending. The potatoes would be brought home in carts and unloaded into a canvas sack held between two pickers and emptied into the store. I remember a cartful of potatoes being horse-drawn out of Gilfach y Dwn Fawr field and one of the wheels going over Joe Bryneithinog's dog. Joe was convinced his dog had been killed. He ran over, fearing the worst. But the dog had been pushed down into the sodden ground and it was pulled out none the worse for wear. From that day, Joe's dog was renamed Resurrection Dog.

Towards the end of the month Father would take some bullocks to Tregaron market. They would be walked the seven miles there and, unless they were sold, they would be walked all the way back as well.

November would begin with the swede and mangold harvest. The root vegetables had to be gathered in before the onset of the first frost. They would be taken to the rickyard and buried in a pit beneath layers of turf and soil. This was done before the farmhands were allowed their annual holidays. This occurred during the traditional hiring period that ended on the thirty-first of October which was Halloween. During their absence I had to help out with the milking and feeding.

This was when the Halloween fairs were held in nearby towns and villages. In our neighbourhood the annual fair would be held on the twenty-fifth of the month when everything would come to a stop. It dated back to the days of the Strata Florida monks and was held on the festival of the Holy Rood. Colloquially it was known as Ffair Rhos, and was the only survivor of five fairs held annually by the monks. The village above Strata Florida is still known as Ffair Rhos or Heath Fair. Only one fair survived, and that ended during the 1960s.

Originally the Ffair Rhos fairs were sheep fairs. It was the monks of Strata Florida who first introduced sheep to this part of Wales, together with shepherding and ear-marking, so I'm particularly proud that our family continued this old tradition. I feel part of that rich heritage.

Gradually these fairs became horse fairs. Back in the 1940s I remember the horse fair held in the morning, with farmers bringing along their horses to sell from as far as the Elan Valley. They would be sold in hand, that is, sold from owner to dealer without the involvement of an auctioneer, with potential buyers discussing and arguing. Sellers would be asked to run their horses along the road, with the buyers closely observing before a bargain was struck. During the afternoon, evening and late into the night, a funfair would be held. By mid evening Terrace Road would be impassable.

The Halloween fairs back then were still recruiting centres for farmhands and maids. At one time farm workers and maids would line up to be inspected by their potential employer. Once a bargain was struck the hired person would receive a small nominal sum as a promissory gesture. According to tradition, any farmhand who had served for seven years on the same farm would be given a heifer by his employer. A maid who had served her employer for seven years would receive a woven woollen bedspread. Alf served with us for twenty-three years, during which time he received three heifers. He would usually sell the heifer back to Father and bank the money.

During my childhood the main Halloween fairs were held in Aberystwyth on three consecutive Mondays. We would all go as a family to the second fair in Dick Jones' taxi. This was the only occasion when Father would buy cigarettes, always Woodbines. Smoking his pipe in the taxi was strictly forbidden as Mam believed that the Ringer's Best pipe tobacco he smoked was too strong for us children to bear. At the fair the Wall of Death would be my main attraction. Dick John and I tried to emulate the motorcyclists' feats on our bikes. We rode our bikes at speed towards the ricks. Needless to say we suffered bruises, but our bruised pride hurt us far more that the falls.

By the end of November the farmhands would be back at work when they would prepare fence posts ready for hedging. And now Christmas was fast approaching. Up to Christmas week we would be busy feeding the cows and horses, hedging, sawing and splitting logs. Then would come the seasonal work of plucking the geese and turkeys. People for miles around would have ordered a bird and, as in the case of picking potatoes, it would be a communal affair with neighbours calling to help. Most of the work would take place after dark. The fire would be lit in the wash house and there would be up to half a dozen people plucking away. After a bird had been plucked, Father would run the bird over the flames to get rid of any remaining stubble and then take it into the house and place it on the stone-topped table in the pantry where it would be disembowelled by Mam and the maid and then dressed. My job would be to write labels and tie them onto the appropriate birds, noting the weight and the names and addresses of the customers. Father would later deliver them in his trap and pony. We would always have a goose on Christmas Day, a turkey on Boxing Day, and another goose on New Year's Day.

Every Christmas we would receive the same presents in our stockings, the standard fare of an orange, a bag of nuts, and a bar of chocolate. Then came a new attraction. Our neighbour David James, who was raised at Pantyfedwen up the road, had become a business success. He had prospered in London and became a millionaire and was knighted. One day, the great man arrived at our school, with his chauffeur

Ned following and carrying bulging sacks full of boxes. We were all called out in turn to receive a present each from the local boy made good. Under Miss Rees' stern gaze we all responded with *'Diolch yn fawr, Syr David!'* In my box was the finest toy steam engine I had ever seen. I still have it.

On Christmas Day we would be woken early to attend the morning service at six. We would see the lights of the lanterns of the worshippers bobbing and getting ever closer as the neighbours made their way from their various farms to the church. It is a sight that I would give anything to witness again. But that would be wishful thinking on my part.

10

A Proper Farmer

IT WAS IN the year before I left school that Father bought his first tractor. He was the last in the district to compromise. It was a Fordson Standard and was, according to Father, the biggest drinker he had ever encountered. In fact, having lingered so long in buying a tractor he decided to buy three all at once. I will have more to say regarding that in another chapter.

What made Father make this major decision was the fact that Alf, the previous autumn, had left to work for the Forestry Commission. Jack had left earlier to work on a neighbouring farm. He had realised that I would soon be leaving school to work at home, making Father surplus to requirements.

By the beginning of the ploughing season Father bought a three-furrowed plough. Visiting us at the time and spending a week's holiday was Father's sister, Aunty Mary Anne, and her husband, Uncle Tom. He drove a car and took to advising Father on his tractor driving. One morning they took the tractor out, with the plough attached – Uncle Tom driving and Father standing behind him. Uncle Tom had the tractor engaged in low gear because of the plough that was in tow.

They intended ploughing stubble on the riverbank. 'No problem!' was Uncle Tom's confident prediction as they left the house. Later that morning Dai Cornwal called and, as he sat there sipping tea, Mam asked him whether he had seen Father and Uncle Tom? Yes, Dai had seen them but hadn't been impressed with their progress. Father had disconnected the plough while Uncle Tom was teaching him to drive. By mid afternoon Father, his pipe smoking like a steam train, was confident enough to go on his own. And, thanks to Uncle Tom, Father and the Fordson forged a deep but unlikely friendship.

A horseman through and through, Father hated cows. He hated milking them even more, even after he bought a milking machine. In those days we had to take the milk up to the village to meet the Milk Marketing Board lorry. Father would take the churns in his trap behind the black cob mare, of the same stock as the famous Billy Boy. The sprightly mare loved nothing more than racing. One morning, Father had loaded the churns, as well as a turkey in a sack to deliver to the landlord of the Black Lion, a Mr Hiscocks. It was a white turkey. For some reason, Hiscocks preferred white turkeys. Off went Father in his trap and pony. On the way he picked up Marged Oliver who had been cleaning at the school and lighting the fire. She sat next to Father and they were proceeding quite nicely until they reached Glasffrwd bridge. Then they heard a commotion and the flapping of wings. The white turkey had freed itself. It flew over the black mare like a feathered helicopter and landed on Dolgoed meadow. This was enough to send the black mare galloping away. She crossed the village square and shot past John David Hopkins the Shoemaker who swore that it must have been chased by a company of Cherokee Indians. On it galloped, the churns toppling and spewing their contents, and Marged thrown on her back with her legs waving in the air exposing her baggy pink bloomers. They didn't stop until they were halfway to Cefn Gaer. Marged never accepted a lift in the trap again! And the Milk Marketing Board decided to send their lorry all the way to our farm to pick up the churns from a newly-erected milk stand, proving that God works in mysterious ways!

It was an easy task for me to take the short step from schoolboy to farmer. It merely meant becoming a full-time rather than a part-time farmer. Although farming was harder physically than it is today, I was in my seventh heaven. There were some tasks that I rather avoided, such as cleaning out the calves' sheds. Another was slicing the stacks of hay using the knife with a twisted handle and tossing an armful of hay in front of the cows. I have a white scar across the tip of one of my thumbs to remind me how sharp that hay knife was.

I still remember how I suffered that accident. One day I was in the hay shed on top of the haystacks slicing hay when a bus stopped opposite the shed. It was a party of visitors to the abbey. As I busied myself sharpening the knife, a group of young and pretty girls got off. I busied myself some more with the sharpening, showing off – but I looked at the girls rather than at the job in hand. Hearing the girls giggling and laughing at my misfortune was worse than the pain of the cut thumb.

After the tractor, the first new-fangled implement to follow must have been the elevator that loaded the hay onto the trailer. It meant less hands and less toil. We tried it out for the first time in a pasture field rich in clover. Off we set, Father driving and me as usual on the trailer. Father drove away with speed as if he was on the open road, puffing nonchalantly on his pipe, not realising that I was being smothered beneath a torrent of falling hay.

Things were just as bad in the hay shed. Uncle Will had introduced an unloading system using hooks running off a rail just beneath the roof. This meant that one man could unload the trailer using a grab that lifted the hay and dumped it wherever was appropriate. The grab was pulled by the blue roan led by Mam. Father would be on the trailer and I would be on top of the stack in the hay shed. Father was so impetuous that he would empty the trailer with just three grabs. The unloading device did not last very long, which suited me fine.

Of the four seasons, my favourite was spring when I would be shepherding – although it meant walking up to thirty miles a day. No one back then would have imagined shepherds using motorbikes or quad bikes. Neither would anyone have imagined sheep lambing in sheds. I remember asking Ned, a neighbour and a good friend, what constituted a good shepherd. He put it succinctly,

'You have to be able to enjoy your own company, to be a good walker and have a good eye, and own a dog that has something other than solid bone between its ears.'

That description still holds true today I believe. I certainly got used to enjoying my own company sitting on a hedgebank or crouching over a sheep or cow waiting for them to give birth in the small hours of the morning.

I would also look forward to the shearing season. And as one who started shearing at twelve years old, I was somewhat experienced by the time I left school. Back then the sheep would be sheared in one shed and the lambs in another. The lamb shearers would be personally chosen by the farmer himself. My turn came at Grofftau, shearing on owner David Morgan's personal request. That day I tried to walk nonchalantly into the lamb shearing shed, hoping that all the others would be looking at me.

A year previously I was at Grofftau shearing and was positioned next to Twm Glangors Fach. Suddenly, a sheep being sheared close by kicked out, sending the shears flying. It embedded itself in Twm's arm. The blood was spouting out. The first to react was Tom Evans, Wellington House. He tore off Twm's shirtsleeve and called for the man in charge of the boiling pitch used for marking the sheep. Tom Evans poured some of the boiling pitch over Twm's arm, cauterising the wound. Twm, although a hard man, was screaming with pain. The hardened pitch took weeks before it peeled off but, when it did, the wound had healed perfectly.

What I really enjoyed during the shearing season was riding on horseback from farm to farm daily. Every shearing shed would bubble with humour and jesting. And the food, of course: the lashings of meat, vegetables and gravy, not forgetting the pudding!

Another activity during shearing period that I enjoyed was breaking in the wild young ponies. Some of these were a problem and offered a challenge, a battle of wits between the pony and myself. I was riding a chestnut pony once after Bryneithinog's shearing and driving some of our strayed sheep home with me. I had broken the pony in but it was still rebellious. I overheard Joe Bryneithinog telling John Gwnden Gwinau that I had quite a task on my hands merely controlling the pony. I took that as a challenge and managed to control the pony and take the stray sheep home.

Following all the socialising that was an integral part of the shearing season, it would be difficult afterwards – especially as tasks now meant working on my own, often in solitude. Still, there was the hay harvest to follow. Father still kept two shire horses and a number of cobs and ponies, as well as the two mares used to mow moorland hay. When a horse needed shoeing, I would take it to Ellis Edwards' smithy three miles away at Ystrad Meurig. Ellis was regarded as a fine blacksmith who never in his life caused a horse an injury. But he was also known for his short temper. He wasn't only a blacksmith; he kept a smallholding and worked as a postman. Like us, he kept Shorthorns, and I still remember a cow that was named Strata Olive Leaf the Third.

Sometimes when I arrived there would already be two or three awaiting their turn. On such occasions Ellis would send me packing, telling me to come back the following day. So I would tie the horse to the smithy door and take a stroll around the Shorthorns. And I would also slip Ellis a bottle of Brown Ale. This would normally pacify him. He would come over to the cowshed for a chat and a few conciliatory words,

'Don't go just yet. I'll find a spare minute or two for you now.'

Father wouldn't let any other blacksmith within a mile of his trotters. Ellis was the only one he trusted to shoe his horses, especially the black cob.

I was at the smithy in 1953 when the Queen was scheduled to visit Aberystwyth as part of her post-Coronation tour around Britain. Mam, for some unknown reason, was a big royalist and she had taken the whole family, apart from me, to town to see Her Majesty. I was an out-and-out socialist, thanks to John Jenkins' left-wing influence. To him the royal family were 'bloody scavengers'. I had taken Ellis the usual bottle of Brown Ale and I had bought one for myself. It was a warm day, and after shoeing our horse he decided to cross the road to Henblas field opposite to sip the beer. I went with him for a chat. The field was crossed by the Carmarthen to Aberystwyth railway line and, as we sat there, the royal train passed by. From where we sat we clearly saw the Queen who must have been puzzled to see two people sitting in the middle of a field drinking Brown Ale and totally ignoring her.

When Mam returned from town she was in a bad mood. Her visit to see the Queen had turned out flat. Because of the size of the crowds, she hadn't even caught a glimpse of Her Majesty. The fact that Ellis and I had seen her passing by through Henblas field was not greatly appreciated.

The corn harvest was approaching and, what with only two shire horses left on the farm, Father decided to adapt the binder so that it could be drawn by the Fordson tractor. When the corn was ripe, off we went, with Father driving and me sitting on the binder. We were then faced with the decision of either stacking the corn later that evening or leaving it until the following morning. It was the day before the annual fair and we had made good progress, meaning that there were sheaves galore to be stacked. Morning dawned and it was pouring with rain. Father departed on his pony to the fair. I decided, despite the rain, to start stacking the sheaves with Charles Cornwal's help. Just before dinner I discovered father's pouch of Ringers Best. We decided to roll a cigarette each, although we had never smoked before. As we stacked the sheaves we smoked two or three each, hoping to make it to the fair in the early evening. We made it there alright but spent most of the time being sick. Father never lost even a pinch of tobacco after that.

The summer of 1953 turned out to be extremely wet and the corn just wouldn't dry. We were forced to leave it in small ricks until the weather turned for the better. Even then we had to demolish the stacks and spread the sheaves all over the fields to dry before bringing them in.

As it was the fair season, we would look forward to visiting surrounding fairs at Tregaron and especially Aberystwyth. I was old enough now to join other local lads on Will Lloyd's bus. It left at 6.30, just after we finished milking. It wouldn't return from Aberystwyth until midnight. The main attraction would be Ron Taylor's boxing booth. Ron would challenge any local lads to climb into the ring to fight one of his boxers, offering £5 to anyone who could last three rounds.

I had become quite adept at the noble art. I would often visit brothers Dai and Ianto at Caemadog to help with the sheep. Dai was the most enthusiastic of the two and he would train me in the basic skills, keeping it a secret from Father of course. Sometimes he would catch me with a haymaker and then goad me with his,

'Get back on your feet, boy!'

We decided – or rather Dai decided – that I was ready to take up Ron Taylor's challenge at Aberystwyth fair. Dai knew the score. Ron's fighters would give their opponents two fairly easy rounds to fire up the audience, but then turn it on in the third. Dai's orders were that I should, in the third round, stick to my opponent like a magnet, crowding him and not giving him a chance to punch.

It went as Dai had predicted. My opponent took it easy for

the first two rounds. At the opening of the third I rushed out of my corner and held on to my opponent, smothering him. And when the final bell rang I was still standing. Dai was delighted and I pocketed a fiver. But for days afterwards I couldn't move. I felt as if I had been through the pulper. And that was my first and my last experience in the boxing ring.

Dai Caemadog was the fittest man I ever met. When we were gathering the flocks, Dai didn't need a horse. He simply ran around the sheep shouting at them while I was on horseback aided by two or three sheepdogs. I once saw him catch up with a wild horse on the run and then punch it to the ground. And he held the horse down while I attached a halter around its head. Should he need to catch the bus in the village two and a half miles away and felt he was late, he would run there all the way without even breaking sweat.

I looked forward to October when the cows would be kept in overnight, all of them tethered making it easier for milking. The drawback was the need to clear out the dung every morning and evening, and taking it by wheelbarrow to be added to the dungheap. For feeding I would have to do the chaffing and pulping and then carry the feed in sacks, a back-breaking task. Sometimes, as a treat, they would be fed barley mixed with treacle. Having carried the mixture, the back of my overcoat would look as if it had been tarred. Should I hang it behind the cowshed door, I would often see Gwenhwyfar, the brindle cow, licking it with gusto.

As well as milking cows we also kept store cattle, usually Shorthorns crossed with a Hereford bull. Father would keep them out until the last January sale, thus ensuring the best possible prices. Keeping them out meant thicker and cleaner coats, making them more attractive to potential buyers. I would feed them daily, carrying sack after sack of chaff, pulp and oatmeal. During rainy weather it would be difficult to reach the feeding pens because of deep mud everywhere, with the cows usually waiting for me to arrive. These were the pre-Wellington boots days with me, according to Dai Cornwal, 'up to my armpits in cow muck'.

I would also drive the cattle, aided by Scott, the red-bellied dog, to their watering holes every day. I remember on one particularly frosty day – the mud hardened like concrete – sending Scott out to drive the cattle to water. Off she went like an express train. Then I heard a squeal, and I ran after Scott only to see her impaled in a sharp ash branch that was embedded like a spear in the frozen mud. The branch had pierced her from belly to back. I carried Scott tenderly to the stall in the stable and laid her down fearing the worst. Luckily, the branch hadn't pierced her through the ribs and was, after all, only skin deep. Within a week Scott was back on duty and none the worse for her ordeal. I later realised that the bitch had been pierced by one of the remnants of the hedge blown in after hedging work. No doubt it had been trampled by the cattle and one end shoved into the ground leaving the other end sticking up like an arrow-head. I discovered a few of them sticking out of the ground like spears.

What made farming interesting to me as a youngster was its ever-changing nature. No two days would be the same. In the autumn, work involving the sheep was particularly varied. As a shepherd I could combine my interests: sheep, dogs and ponies without anyone interfering with my daily tasks. The mountain was open land without any boundaries between us and the Elan Valley in one direction; Llanwrtyd in the other and Rhandirmwyn to the south. I never felt lonely up in the hills. Now and then I'd see in the far distance one of the Cerrig Cyplau brothers driving sheep. Then, on another occasion, I'd see Dick John up on Moel Prysgau, Ned up at Gorast lake or Tom Blaenglasffrwd heading for home over Pen Bwlch.

Pen Bwlch, to me, was a magical place, especially in summer. From its summit, reaching some 1,200 feet above sea level, I could see a panorama of Cardiganshire down as far as the Preseli Hills in Pembrokeshire. Dai Cornwal, on the other hand, hated the place because it was always cold there, cold enough according to Dai to 'freeze a flea to a cow's belly'.

Sheepdogs were an obvious interest, and through that interest and following sheepdog trials I made many friends over the years, one in particular in Dai Jones Llanilar. We have travelled together far and wide over the years competing, judging and merely enjoying ourselves. I have always kept Welsh sheepdogs, both brindle and red, and all of them energetic and lively.

Then, at the local trials, I was asked to help out moving the sheep for the various competitors. The giants of the trialling circuit back then included D.C. Morgan, Trefenter; John Evans, Llanybydder; Dai Daniel, Ystradgynlais; John Evans, Magor; and John Jones, Trawsfynydd. I was busy moving the sheep one day in Pontrhydfendigaid when I was approached by the judge, Mr Jarman from Carno, who suggested I should turn to keeping the Scotch Collie. I took his advice and that's what really started me off. Little did I realise then that I would move to Meirionethshire where I would become very friendly with the Jarman family.

As much as I enjoy seeing dogs working in tandem with their handlers at trials, I still believe that a sheepdog is not really in its element unless it is working on the open mountain. I can't imagine a better feeling than being out on the mountain on a windy morning in autumn with the flock running amok, only for the dog to patiently round them up and bring them to the shepherd's feet. Perhaps a shepherd becomes a natural part of his or her environment, with the peaty waters in the soil beneath his or her feet entering the bloodstream. I may be romanticising, but I believe in such fanciful thoughts.

But let's forget the mountain for a minute and turn to a young man's leisure activities outside his work. Thanks mainly to the local vicar, John Aubrey, there was something or other organised at the church hall every week, especially during the winter months. The hall was of a simple construction, functional rather than luxurious, with wooden chairs, a stage and two anterooms. Every autumn for a fortnight, a professional drama company from the Midlands would bring the best of repertory performances to us, with a different play six nights a week. It was a family company led by Jimmy James. The plays were classics, from *The Winslow Boy* to *A Streetcar Named Desire*, every performance ending with a comic sketch. There were melodramas too, like *The Murder in the Red Barn*. There were murders galore, with the perpetrators hanged. I just couldn't understand how some of these actors who had been murdered or hanged were walking around the village the following day! I remember Marged Williams asking me one night on her way out where all these dead people would be buried!

During the day the actors, who lodged at Llys Meurig,

would be walking around learning their lines. One was Mary Wimbush. Another, Ray Cooney, became a leading member of the Whitehall Theatre with Brian Rix.

John Aubrey, our colourful and dynamic vicar, was right at the heart of the community. He was very supportive of Miss Rees, our headmistress. During the fishing season he would come over to fish on our land. Should Father ask him how he was getting on he would answer,

'Tommy, fishing is just like saving souls, it is always an uphill task.'

On one occasion the vicar forgot that he had left his car near the riverbank. The river was in flood and, by the time he called to retrieve his car, the water was halfway up the doors and Father had to fetch the tractor to tow his car to dry land using a new rope he had just bought from the Co-op. The engine had choked and Father had to tow him all the way back to the village.

Things started off promisingly – Father and I on the tractor and Aubrey steering the car. Unfortunately, he put the car in gear hoping it would start. Unfortunately, it proved too much for the new rope and it snapped. Father turned to me saying,

'That bloody vicar will use up all my new rope if he isn't careful.'

He hadn't realised that Aubrey was standing behind him.

'Don't you worry, Tommy,' he said, 'you'll get another rope in heaven.'

'The problem is, vicar,' said Father, 'I'll need it long before I get that far!'

I was born at a time when religion was central to community life. And Aubrey more than played his part. His weakness was the bottle, but he was such a lovely man that his parishioners turned a blind eye. He would stride around the village wearing his large black clerical hat at an angle. Denomination mattered little to Aubrey, and he would tend to anyone and everyone. He was among those who founded Pontrhydfendigaid's football club in 1947 and can be seen in a central position in old team photographs.

His house was packed with books and he was always ready to lend me any volume I wanted. He even helped us out on the farm when Father was ill and he would often be seen helping some of the elderly to carry the coal in. John Aubrey was a true Christian whose creed and daily life were as one.

Aubrey was instrumental in providing films at the church hall on Saturday nights, hired from a company in Aberystwyth. The village's electricity supply was spasmodic as the turbine up at Cwm Mawr was not very dependable. It had been built by Danny Rees, an eccentric genius, and, as the flood in the river fluctuated, so did the electricity supply. I remember watching *The Cruel Sea*, during which there were four breaks in transmission. We young men welcomed these breaks. During these periods, with the hall in darkness, we would chat up the local girls. Unfortunately, what with the early milking the following morning in time to catch the milk lorry, I seldom took the opportunity to walk anyone home.

11

In the Club

TWO HOURS DURING one's lifetime doesn't amount to much. But it is long enough to lead to changing one's life completely, as I discovered one October night in 1950. I was sitting on the parapet of the bridge in the village chatting with Dick Davies. Then, John Jenkins stopped by, and without any preamble told both of us to accompany him. We did. No one argued with John Jenkins.

John took us to the church hall where Councillor Emrys Lloyd, together with a complete stranger, was addressing a crowd of young people. Emrys introduced the stranger as Aelwyn Jones. He, apparently, was the organiser of the Cardiganshire branch of the Federation of Young Farmers' Clubs. He outlined the work of the Movement and expressed his opinion that the Pontrhydfendigaid area would be perfect for establishing a branch. Even before he sat down, John Jenkins proposed creating such a branch. And he proposed I should be chairman! Talk about being thrown in at the deep end! The other officers were then elected and I found myself sitting at the end of a long table, with John Jenkins calling for hush so that the new chairman could speak. What was I to do? I had no idea. I had never been chairman of any committee in my life. John whispered in my ear,

'Call on Aelwyn Jones to address the new branch.'

I did, and things proceeded nicely as we started to discuss our forthcoming programme. And so I survived my very first meeting of the Ystrad Fflur Young Farmers' Club. But, early the following night, I was knocking on John Jenkins' front door informing him that I was tendering my resignation. He invited me in, sat me down and told me,

'No one who falls into a pond gives in just because he can't swim. Don't be such a coward!'

An hour and two cups of tea later, and I was back in the fold. Not only was I branch chairman of the YFC again, I had also half-promised to join the Labour Party!

John had been an exile in the south Wales coalfields and still waved the Red Flag. My parents, both staunch Liberals, feared I was being led astray. I would consult with John regularly regarding committee protocol. He always stressed the need for an agenda and the importance of never sitting on the fence. I still cherish all the wisdom that this old miner taught me.

One of our immediate priorities was to find a suitable meeting place. Again, it was John who came to our aid. There was a house being offered for sale in Teifi Street. Five of us became trustees and invested £100 each in paying the purchase price of £500. The ground floor would be a committee room and there was a loft we could use for storage. Additionally, Mary Roberts, who lived next door, agreed to light a fire for us prior to our meetings.

Gradually other clubs heard of our existence and we were invited to join them in social evenings. We would travel, five or six of us, in Will Lloyd's taxi driven by Dick Davies. Known to all as Dick Bach, ironically because of his gigantic size, he was himself a member. Despite his formidable appearance

Dick was always dependable and full of mischief. Back then the Methodist chapel would stage an eisteddfod in the vestry every Christmas night. Once, in the middle of a singing competition as the minister who was compering called for hush, Dick broke wind loudly. He immediately turned around and addressed two elderly sisters sitting behind him and berated them,

'Shame on you!'

The two innocent sisters didn't know where to look. For all his strength, Dick died young – before his fiftieth birthday – depriving the village of a great character.

Despite all the enjoyment, the club was imbued with a strong competitive element. Competitions were to be enjoyed, yes, but they were there to be won as well. Our public speaking teams and individuals were particularly able. We reached our peak at the Kings Hall, Aberystwyth, in 1956 when our senior team was adjudged best in Wales. I felt saddened that John Jenkins hadn't been there to witness it. He would have loved it, although he would have found some fault or other to keep our feet on the ground. To the great majority of us members, the club was our college. Not only did we receive tuition in all kinds of subjects, not least gaining the confidence of standing up in public, it also made us feel we belonged to other young people throughout Wales and beyond.

The County Rally was an annual highlight that involved weeks or even months of preparation. I was away more often than I would be at home, and every time he happened to see me around the place Father would ask me if I was a visitor! The highlight for us would be the stock judging competition. It also meant the added attraction – to those that made it to the county team – of being given a free trip to the Dairy Show in London. I was lucky to make the county team more than once, judging both milk and store cattle. Just as interesting to me would be the opportunities to visit various farms and learn from those visits. We would be overseen by John Lloyd from the Ministry of Agriculture who specialised on farm stock. His particular favourites were the Shorthorns. He wouldn't hear one word of criticism of the breed. His advice to us every time we were about to compete was,

'Be true to your own judgment. Ignore anyone else's advice.'

I was lucky enough to do well in the judging and shearing competitions. Back then the Royal Welsh Show was still peripatetic. I was learning to drive when I headed up to Bangor to judge the Welsh Blacks on behalf of the county team. Prior to the show John Lloyd had taken us to visit Morfa Mawr with Llew Phillips to inspect the herd. Morfa Mawr was a Ministry (MAFF) experimental farm on the coast at Llannon, and Llew Phillips the publicity officer for MAFF. Uncle Will was my experienced driver on the visit to Bangor, and Uncle John Morgan also accompanied us. Uncle Will directed me to drive via Blaenau Ffestiniog and over the Crimea Pass. Uncle John Morgan's comment on the surrounding fields was,

'Terrible land. You couldn't even grow a hedge here! No wonder they need stone walls.'

Another great supporter of us Young Farmers' was Reg Evans, head of the Ministry farm at Crosswood. He would welcome us there at any time, even evenings and weekends, ensuring that there was stock there for us to inspect whenever we wished. Luckily for us, another member of staff at

Crosswood, Jim Holmes, lived in Pontrhydfendigaid and he was always ready to help.

Another competition we specialised in was the drama competition, taking us all over Wales. I was fortunate enough to have been involved with drama at school, thanks to Miss Rees. Then we managed to recruit a true professional, Gwynne Hughes Jones, whose brother Alwyn was also very much involved in acting. Alwyn became known as Mr Gwyther in the Welsh soap opera *Pobol y Cwm*.

Gwynne was a stickler, especially for promptness. He gave us only a few days to learn our lines. Here again, one of John Jenkins' sayings was most appropriate,

'If you want to perform in public, make sure you have skin as thick as an elephant's hide.'

You needed it when Gwynne was in charge. But he was being cruel to be kind, and without him we would not have been anything like as successful as we became. We regularly represented Cardiganshire in the all-Wales finals. We represented Wales as well in the Welsh Youth Drama Festival organised by the British Drama Society. It was held at Newtown Pavilion on a bitterly cold night in February 1954. One of our members, Byron, was sick all night and we had to leave him at an Aberystwyth hospital on our way home. He was suffering with appendicitis and was operated upon the following day. Byron was another member we lost young, leaving a great void.

Gwynne, having contributed all he could, advised us to go our own way as we had by now the necessary experience and know-how. He passed the reins on to me and I merely took over the talent that Gwynne had nurtured. We now widened our horizons by competing at the Urdd drama competition.

We won the national drama competition three times at the beginning of the 1960s.

My greatest moment came by default. I was playing the part of Judas Iscariot in the play *Y Chweched Awr* [The Sixth Hour]. It was 1960, and the national finals were held at the Kings Hall in Aberystwyth. The adjudicator was Mary Lewis of Llandysul, a formidable drama critic and judge. She always watched like a hawk and knew the scripts of every presentation almost word for word. I had warned the prompter to be at the ready. But, for the only time in my life, I froze. I felt as if an age had passed before I recalled the missing words. After the curtain fell I apologised to the others. I had blown it.

Then came the adjudication. Mary Lewis declared that the highlight of our play was the way Judas Iscariot had delayed one of his responses. I had, she said, created unexpected tension that was most effective. And so a night to forget turned into a night to remember. I won the cup for best actor. And I never told Mary Lewis the truth. I left her in blissful ignorance!

Producing plays in Pontrhydfendigaid was a pleasure. Members always turned up on time for the twice-weekly rehearsals. Not only were we lucky in our actors, but we also had set builders, prompters, make-up artistes and the like. It was so different back then, whereas today a producer has new technology to call upon.

If it was at Aberystwyth that we witnessed our great moment on stage, it was our return journey from the Urdd National Eisteddfod at Ruthin in 1962 that we had our most memorable debacle. The play we presented there involved a forest scene, meaning we needed a trailer full of props towed by a Land Rover. Having won, we naturally celebrated late into the night before going for home. I was to go out gathering sheep at daybreak. Dick John was driving, and tiredness got the better of him and suddenly the Land Rover found itself in a field. The trailer hadn't overturned but it had spilled props everywhere. Dick had badly hurt his hand and I had a bad back. We retrieved as many of the props as was possible and started looking for a gate we could exit through. Somehow or other we made it home. And yes, thanks to a very sympathetic pony, I did manage to gather the sheep later that morning.

The Young Farmers' Club contributed immensely to the life of young people in the neighbourhood, providing us with more than any college could have offered. John Jenkins was right back then when he urged me to join.

'One day,' he said, 'you will thank me for giving you the chance to place your feet beneath the table.'

I know I'm late in saying this John, but thank you.

1 2

Characters

THE LIFE OF the neighbourhood moved on inexorably. It does little good in looking back longingly but it is impossible to completely close the door on memories and on the characters that shaped them.

One of these was Dafydd Hughes the Stonemason who always carried his canvas bag full of the tools of his trade on his back. Like so many villagers back then, Dafydd kept two or three Shorthorn cows. He was nicknamed *Oblegid*, meaning 'Because'. He would introduce that word into practically every sentence he uttered. He worked for us fairly regularly and taught me the rudiments of building stone walls. He would often advise me,

'Never pick up a stone unless you mean to use it,' or 'The stonemason's greatest tools are his eyes.'

I remember Dafydd obtaining a radio, or rather a wireless as it was known back then, a device that was totally alien to him. Every morning he would listen to the weather forecast. Then he would pop in next door to ask Tommy the Post what *his* radio had prophesied!

He had the gift of the water dowser. Using a forked hazel twig, he could locate underground springs. Father called him over one day to locate a spring on our land. Within an hour Dafydd had located a source, announcing grandly,

'This is where it lies, Tommy! There's enough water here to drown Aberystwyth.'

A week later Dafydd and I started digging at the designated spot. We dug for days and the only water that ensued was the sweat from our brows. In fairness to Dafydd, he helped me close the hole and later he was successful in finding water. So all was forgiven.

His ambition was to win a red card at the local village show with one of his Shorthorns. I always knew when one of his cows had calved. He would spend most of his time in the cowshed. He would show me the new calf with the words,

'This is it, the champion. No one will beat this one.'

He died however without achieving his great ambition.

Another great character was Rhys Jones, a local musician who adopted the bardic name *Alaw Fflur*. He had his own choir for many years, but he is best remembered as curator of Strata Florida Abbey. His exalted position led to his being awarded a royal honour. He would lead visitors around the abbey, regaling them with both fact and fiction. By the end not even Rhys himself could distinguish the one from the other. One day, one of the visitors came across a jawbone. Rhys said it must have belonged to one of the princes who were connected with the abbey. Among those present was a vet, and he corrected Rhys, explaining that it was a bone from a cow's leg!

Every autumn he would ferment nettle wine. One night, I foolishly helped him consume two bottles. For some reason, on my way home my bike wanted to take a different route to me! Rhys was also an officer in the Home Guard and many were the occasions that Jack and I watched secretly from the cowshed loft while he put Alf through his paces, marching and drilling. He also gave Alf singing lessons, which prompted Mat the maid to opine that Rhys was more likely to be able to teach Alf to sing in tune that to cause Hitler any reason for losing sleep!

Rhys was a great believer in the spiritual afterlife and regularly held séances. Only true believers were allowed to attend, meaning that it took a lot of persuading before he allowed me to be present. I had to inform him in advance the name of the departed family member I wished to contact. Come the big night, and I settled down quietly with the rest and on my best behaviour. Rhys' front room was lit with candles as he invited my long-lost relative to contact him. As he concentrated deeper and deeper, I lunged at the woman sitting next to me, grabbing her on the knee. She jumped off her seat screaming, and knocked a candle off the table. I was immediately expelled and banned from attending any future séances. The following day the woman I had frightened apologised to me, saying that I had probably reacted through a randy old uncle of hers!

Another character who provided hours of pleasure was George Cornwal, not my former school friend but rather his father. He was a lengthsman with the County Council and I still can't fathom how one man with only a spade, pick and a sickle managed to keep his patch so tidy. I presume his home, Cornwal, was named by a Cornish miner who came to these parts to try his luck. George's great gift was to lengthen a five-minute story into a half-hour epic. Years later, Ronnie Corbett earned thousands for doing the same thing. George would inevitably begin with,

'Have you heard the latest?'

Even before I had answered, he was away.

'Wait a minute now. It was yesterday morning. No, I hadn't reached Caemadog gate by then. Where was I now? I had hung my lunch bag on a branch of the old oak tree above the road when I felt like having a cup of tea. No, that couldn't be true, because Dick Jones had just passed on his way to pick up Marged Berthgoed to meet the Tregaron bus. The bus leaves at five to twelve. So I couldn't have had a cup of tea, as lunchtime was only twenty minutes away and Tommy the Postman hadn't yet gone past. Why did I reach for the lunch bag? Now I remember. I felt like filling my pipe, and I knew I had left my tobacco pouch in the bag. Yes, and as I did so I saw Tommy approaching on his bike from Graig Fach hill.'

I was now itching to go on my way but I would humour him,

'And what did Tommy have to say?'

'That's exactly what I was about to tell you. But you know as well as I how slow Tommy is with his stories. He only had to call at Frongoch and Troedrhiw with nothing of importance in their envelopes, so he said.'

'But what about the latest? What were you going to tell me?'

'Well, there you are, it was to be expected I suppose, although whether it will be a success, no one knows. And how long it will take to install it is another question.'

'George, what is about to be installed?'

'Oh, didn't I tell you? The electricity supply is coming soon. Mind you, it will be strange without the old Tilley lamp. Expensive it will be, I'll bet. Imagine it, a flame in a glass bulb, according to Tommy. What is the world coming to?'

Yes, George Edwards, Cornwal – the lengthsman who

lovingly looked after two roads along two valleys as if they were his very own. In a way, they were.

George Cornwal wouldn't have hated anyone. He never harboured an ounce of hatred. But even he could have made an exception of Twm Gargoed. Mind you, you could never accuse Twm of being prejudiced. Twm found fault in everyone. Twm was a small, light-footed man, his cap always worn low above his eyes. Being that he was so short, he had to bend backwards before he could look anyone in the eyes. Under his cap he kept bits of the *Welsh Gazette*. Every time he fancied rolling himself a cigarette, he would tear a piece of the paper for rolling his tobacco. Dai Cornwal would always harass him, telling him to buy proper cigarette paper. His explanation was,

'By using bits of the *Welsh Gazette*, I can enjoy a smoke and read the paper at the same time.'

There existed bad blood between Twm and one of his nearest neighbours, Ianto Caemadog, on account of Twm's sheep straying onto Ianto's land. But one spring it was Caemadog sheep that had strayed into Twm's corn. Ianto's response was to tell Twm to put up a fence.

'Why should I?' asked Twm. 'Your sheep could find their way through the eye of a needle.'

To which Ianto replied,

'The good Lord was ever so wise in creating a man as idiotic as you in such a small-sized body!'

They lived and died sworn enemies to the last.

Another small, light-footed man was Iori Williams, or Iori Bach to all who knew him. His great gift was whistling. He was Pontrhydfendigaid's answer to Ronnie Ronalde. He could emulate a blackbird, or any other songbird come to that. He even performed on radio programmes. He firmly believed that, come television, he would make a fortune. But it wasn't to be.

He then turned to singing. He was fated, he believed, to be 'the second David Lloyd'. Unfortunately, he never even became the first Iori Williams. He had his own tutor, a retired headmaster from Tregaron. But they spent more time at the bar of the Red Lion than they did practising.

He worked for us for a while and became interested in horse racing. He had the right physique to be a jockey, but not the application. He would be regularly thrown. It happened once at Pontrhydfendigaid show when he landed in hospital. But back he came, the perpetual optimist.

I remember him once in our hay field, Father having sent him to gather in the hay while he and I prepared the baler. When we reached the field Iori was on the side-rake but had gone the wrong way round, meaning that much of the outer swathes of hay were tossed onto the hedges. When Mat the maid asked him why he had not spotted his mistake he replied,

'I decided to provide more shelter for you and your future vicar!'

Mat, at the time, was walking out with a young man who was at St John's College in Ystrad Meurig where ecclesiastical students were taught.

Iori would change his ambitions more often than he would change his shirt. He turned to fishing, buying all the paraphernalia. He caught nothing much except a cold and soon abandoned his piscatorial interests. He then turned to running dogs in sheepdog trials. Again, it was just a passing fancy.

To Iori there was a fine line between fact and fiction and Iori crossed it regularly. He would approach total strangers in the bar of the Black Lion where he would pass himself off as a local farm owner. He would invite them over to see the farm, even to ride or shoot, and would be royally entertained by the strangers in the bar. Iori would promise to pick them up at the pub the following morning. Suffice it to say that they would never see 'that nice Mr Williams' again. He died far too young, an exile in Aberystwyth after having taken up sea angling.

Whereas Iori was a fantasist, Tom Norris, on the other hand, was conscientious to a fault. Raised in a Dr Barnado's home somewhere in England, he was sent to Wales as a farm worker where he learnt the language. Well, a kind of pidgin Welsh. He worked at Grofftau, Hafod y Rhyd and Allt Ddu. He was thin, tall and ungainly, and rode a bike until he bought a Bantam motorcycle.

Once a year the Dr Barnado's collection boxes would reach the village and Tom would always contribute a five pound note, which was almost equal to a month's pay. One day he ran into our house calling to Mam,

'Mrs Arch, have you got some proper money I can use in the kiosk?'

'Yes,' answered Mam. 'Has anything happened at Grofftau?'

'Yes,' answered Tom. 'Mrs Arch, there is a terrible place there. The red cow is in a state. Wants to give birth to a calf but doing nothing but mooing and peeing. I have to phone the vet.'

The vet arrived and the calf was duly born.

At shearing Tom's task was to wrap the fleeces and he was

expert at the work thanks to his long, spindly arms. Some of the youngsters who took the fleeces from him would try to rush him, but Tom would be ahead of them every time.

His motorcycle driving test remains a part of local legend. Having gone to Lampeter for his test, he was back on the farm within half an hour. When Dai Allt Ddu asked him how come he was home so soon, Tom answered,

'I don't quite know. The tester told me to ride around the back of the mart. I did, but I couldn't see him anywhere, so I drove home. I don't know whether I passed or not.'

Yes, Tom Norris, the orphan who tried his very best and succeeded. A good and faithful servant.

A local eccentric who lived across the river was Danny Bronberllan or, to us, Danny Low Gear. On his daily visits to the village and back, you would have to concentrate hard before realising he was moving at all. Always at his side was his lethargic greyhound, and it was a constant dilemma whether Danny walked in time with the greyhound or whether the greyhound walked in time with Danny.

Danny was a quiet, kind man. Yet, despite his slowness, he would never stop to talk. He kept inching along. We found ourselves either always in front of him or always behind him. Being both slow and evasive at the same time took some doing. But Danny Low Gear managed it. He only had two true friends, his faithful greyhound and a surly-looking goat. One day, the goat made its way across the river into the school yard where it chased us around, jumping on our backs. Country children like us knew what it was all about. We had seen cows do it. They were merely following the call of nature. But, for Anna, the London evacuee, this was something new. She ran away up the road chased by the goat. She ended up in our house, hiding halfway up the mantle chimney. At the time I'm sure that Anna would rather have faced the wrath of the Luftwaffe than Danny Low Gear's goat!

Our land was crossed by a footpath that ran from the nearby old Bronberllan lead mine all the way to Gelligron, a large expanse of heathland some three miles away. In effect, it connected the sites of the two abbeys as well, the original still known as Old Abbey and the ruins of the abbey that succeeded it where we lived. This path was regularly used by the small crofters who lived on Gelligron for their daily toil to the mines. Their homes would have been one of the one-night houses that proliferated between the seventeenth and nineteenth centuries when homeless people were allowed to build houses on common land. They were allowed only by being completed overnight, with smoke rising from the chimney by dawn. The new owner would then throw an axe from the front door as far as possible. The spot where the axe hit the ground would be the new home's land boundary.

With the demise of lead mining, the houses were left empty and even their remains have now long disappeared, save for a very few. The lead miners mostly headed south to mine for coal. One or two remained on Bronberllan heath. One such croft was Gwndwn Gwinau, where John Rees Jones lived almost all his life there on his own. John was a short, solid man who was born handicapped with one leg shorter than the other. When he wasn't on horseback he would hobble around on crutches. He would frequent every shearing in the district and he would always be the one who would tend to the sheep that needed dosing against a disease known as fluke. He would kneel by the side of the sheep and push a pill the size of an acorn down its throat with the tip of one long finger. John's dosing finger was a local legend. I remember Ianto Caemadog threatening Twm Gargoed once with the words,

'Mind yourself or I'll get John Gwndwn Gwinau to stuff a pill so far down your throat until it appears out of your arse!'

John kept his own flock of Torwen sheep on the heath. He would always be seen there on horseback. I remember him once delivering a white gander in a basket for Mam. I had gone up to Waunwen to bring in the cows for evening milking and I joined him on the path. Suddenly, one of the young cows began chasing us. John's horse bolted, throwing John and the gander in a heap. He was soon back in the saddle none the worse for wear. And the gander survived as well.

John was a deacon in the local Methodist chapel and always attended in a black homespun dark grey suit with a double gold chain across his waistcoat. At the branch chapel in Glanrafon, John ruled the roost. He was treasurer of the annual competitive concert. Before he died he wrote a book on local history.

When Father, back in the 1950s, decided to buy a tractor, he took me with him to the tractor centre in Aberystwyth. No two people ever knew less about tractors than Father and I. We looked at the tractors on show and Father decided on a Fordson. But, just in case it happened to fail to start some morning, he decided he needed some insurance. And so he bought three!

The three tractors duly arrived by lorry, or rather by lorries. One of the lorry drivers was unable to comprehend why two of us needed three tractors. The following morning we couldn't start even one of the three, so we called Danny Rees. Danny was an unsung engineering genius but an utter eccentric. Today he would be in the vanguard of the attempt to send a man to Mars. He ran local buses and built a turbine to supply the village with electricity. He spoke quietly and softly but would only answer an emergency call in his own good time. I cycled over to see him and provided him with the necessary details. Shortly before midnight the next night, Father heard a noise out in the yard. It was Danny chuckling to himself outside the cart house where the tractors were kept.

'What's up?' asked Father.

'Can't you see?' answered Danny. 'The tractor was pregnant! There's another two there now!'

Father left him there chuckling but, the following morning, all three tractors were started successfully. But we only used the one. Danny was loath to reveal the cause of any mechanical problems. He called with us one night around 10.30, asking me to accompany him to Penddolfawr to attend to another mechanical problem. This time it was to do with a hay scuffler. He wanted me to hold the candle while he took off one of the wheels. The farmer, Uncle Rhys, was in bed.

'I'm afraid he's in for bad news,' said Danny. 'This is going to cost him, and you know how stingy he is.'

Danny removed the broken part but was back the following afternoon. He had forged a new part and the scuffler was soon working as good as new. Yes, if Danny was with us today, he would be a famous engineer, as long as it didn't mean working mornings.

This was around the time when the Forestry Commission poked its nose into the Glasffrwd valley. Most of

Pantyfedwen, the nearest farm, was sold off. It was there, at the small mansion, that Sir David James' family had farmed prior to his move to London where he made his fortune. I can only remember seeing his mother, Catherine James, once when she visited Mam. In fact, it was impossible to see her face as she always hid behind a black veil. It was said that even Ned, her chauffeur, had only seen her face once when he had to brake hard on Rhiw Dywyll to avoid hitting Will Blaenglasffrwd's horse and cart.

'What did she look like?' asked George Cornwal. 'Did she come out to give Will a telling off?'

'No,' answered Ned, 'but her face came out – right through the veil!'

From the sale of Pantyfedwen, some fifty acres of land were retained for someone to continue farming, and a husband and wife were duly installed there. Mr and Mrs Gutteridge, an English couple, had lived for a while above Machynlleth. Years later Mari and I moved to that area to live and met members of the family there.

Oliver Gutteridge kept a few cows and poultry and also a shire horse he used to drag tree trunks for the Forestry Commission. The harness continually broke, meaning that he would be constantly begging for spare parts. We became close friends and saw a lot of each other.

One spring, Guttreridge decided to sow a field of oats, with the main objective of feeding his shire horse. I helped him with the sowing and the subsequent rolling to facilitate the future use of the binder when harvesting. However, a big storm broke around the beginning of September and the oats were flattened. Using the binder was impossible, so I promised to help him, each of us using a scythe. When he arrived at the field he was also carrying a sack. I soon discovered that the sack was full of Brown Ale in bottles. At every headland we stopped for a drink. Every time we resumed I would be leading. But, as we progressed, I could hear the swish of Gutteridge's scythe getting nearer and nearer to my heels, so I decided to change the order. However, we eventually completed the task, having also emptied around three dozen bottles of Brown Ale. And, as we entered the yard at Pantyfedwen, the horse and cart demolished one of the gate pillars.

Then Gutteridge had a brainwave. He ordered pre-Christmas turkeys, picking up the chicks from the railway station in his car. The poor chicks had been in cardboard boxes during the train journey. As a result, the boxes were wet and fragile, meaning that Gutteridge's back seat was a mess. The car stank for weeks afterwards.

Christmas was nearing and it was time to kill and defeather the turkeys. And naturally he asked for my help. One evening, after the milking, I called. He was waiting for me. So was a crate full of Brown Ale. He did the killing while I did the plucking. Soon the cowshed was awash with blood. It was exactly like a scene from *The Murder in the Red Barn* I had seen at the church hall. A few years later he departed the area, an Englishman who had been totally accepted by all of us who got to know him.

I referred earlier to Will Blaenglasffrwd. Will, with his two brothers and a sister, lived at the head of the Glasffrwd valley, the road leading up to Abergwesyn. It was a mountain croft but Will would refute that assertion by growing black oats, potatoes and swedes on three or four fields salvaged from the surrounding bogland.

Will's brother Tom was tall and sturdy, but Jack was retarded, never leaving home. Marged, the sister, tended them all. Tom was versed in the mountain ways. He used terms and phrases long forgotten by everyone else. Tom was a true mountain man with a memory as old as the hills themselves. Sometimes we would meet, dismount and talk while our horses lazily grazed nearby. He would tell me the exact date when the cudweed had appeared in previous years. Or, he would gaze upwards and predict the weather for the next few days. He was always right. He was versed in the movement of the flocks and could tell me what direction the wind was about to take. He hated the thick fog that hung over the streams, as that would precede snow. He was meticulous in caring for his boots, greasing them with goose fat every night. When it came to notching lambs' ears, Tom was the master. He used a penknife that was sharp enough for shaving with.

But Will was the family spokesman. He attended chapel. He would just as faithfully attend the Tregaron weekly mart. And when it came to visiting neighbours, it was always Will. When fair day came, and the Pontrhydfendigaid agricultural show day, Will would be there. Occasionally, on such occasions, he would sip a pint or two in the small bar at the Black with Father.

The small bar, *Y Bar Bach* as it was known, was forbidden territory to all but the chosen few. The only way for an outsider to be allowed in was by invitation. I will never forget the night that Ianto John beckoned me in.

'Come in here and join us,' he said.

I did, proudly.

Every spring, without exception, before we took to sowing

our own land, Will would arrive at the farmyard with his horse and cart to borrow the swede drill. Within a few days I would have to go up there to fetch it back for our own use, Will swearing blind he had just finished using it. He wanted to give the impression that his patch of swedes was larger than ours!

It was the same at the Blaenglasffrwd shearing. Will deliberately slowed everything down to give the impression that he had far more sheep than he really owned. Today I feel privileged to have known people like Will and Tom Roberts, Blaenglasffrwd. I remember my old pal John Nantllwyd telling me once,

'Mountain men; mountain manners.'

It was a perfect description of such men as Will and Tom.

Those were the days of the tramps; itinerants who moved to do occasional work from farm to farm. One of these was Jim Daley, a two-yard-tall Irishman who could be rather wild. It was said that he took to the road following an incident back home when he took his father's cows to market. He sold them for ready money but spent it all with his friends at the pub. He was too afraid to go home and face his father, so he started walking and just carried on.

He would work for us for some three days at a time before spending his earnings on beer and moving on. He could be fierce in his drink, but upon sobering would settle down again. Once, while with us, and not having quite sobered, he was pushing a barrow load of cow dung. He had overloaded it to such an extent that it toppled over, spilling everything and breaking to bits in the bargain. Jim took it out on the white cow. The cow kicked out, catching Jim in a most delicate part of his anatomy and leaving him gasping and sobering in the straw.

Jim was a master at hedging and, as we had two miles of hedges bordering the road, he would be given the job every autumn. One day I called him to his dinner and found him in one of his bad moods. He had the wanderlust, and demanded his money so that he could leave. He picked up his canvas sack containing his tools and swung it over his shoulder. Among the tools was an axe and the blade cut through the sack and entered his back. I led him home, blood soaking into his boots. We had to call Dr Davies from Tregaron to treat him. He was placed on his front on the kitchen table, Alf and I holding an arm each. The doctor poured a little whiskey over the blade and the wound and gave the rest to Jim to drink. Then the doctor pulled suddenly on the axe and it was out, blood hitting the ceiling. The wound was stitched and Jim had to keep to his bed for a fortnight while I tended him. Then he got up and continued working as before. Following his accident we became good friends. He would often talk about me to others with the words,

'Young Arch is the best bloke around.'

According to Dr Davies I had done exactly the right thing in leaving the axe in his back. Had I taken it out he would have bled to death.

Another 'gentleman of the road' who would call with us was known as Harry Lauder. He and Jim were sworn enemies. Harry would confine himself to gardening work, just enough to buy a few pints before moving on again. I have never seen anyone who could eat so much. He was always willing to lie so that he could have even more. One morning he had already eaten a hearty breakfast before reaching us. He was sleeping in the cowshed when I arrived. He woke up and went to the house swearing to Mam that he hadn't eaten for days. Mam, of course, believed him.

Later that day I went over to Dolebolion for the threshing. There, Dai the farmhand asked me why I had been so tetchy that morning. He went on to explain that Harry had called begging for a bite to eat and had told Dai that I had sent him packing without any breakfast! The following day he related the same story at Penwernhir, but this time blaming Dolebolion for refusing him breakfast. And so he went on telling his tall tales and eating his way around.

Once he was helping Mam in the garden when they started discussing the graves in the nearby cemetery. Harry had heard that the graves were not being dug deep enough. Mam thought nothing more about it. But Harry wasn't happy. That evening, he climbed over the wall into the cemetery where there was an open grave. Harry jumped in. He bent down to measure the depth with his eyes. Unbeknown to him, a couple from the village were canoodling at the lynch gate. Ted Edwards and Elen Jenkins were lost to love when Harry, in the twilight, stood up. They ran for their lives, while Harry got out quite unconcerned with it all.

Another tramp who would call regularly was a man who was known as Swift. Apparently he didn't want anyone to know his Christian name. Why, I have no idea, as we all knew it was Harry. He would seldom be seen over the winter as he would, so it was said, toss a stone through a shop window around the beginning of November so that he would be thrown in jail for a few months. Swift had apparently fought in the war, only to return home to London to find his home bombed and his family killed.

Why he took to the roads of Wales, no one knew. He would frequent all the shearing around here, mostly employed with gathering the fleeces. Tricks would be played on him, with some of the youngsters planting stones among the fleeces. He would mutter away but never retaliated.

Once, at Tywi Fechan, as the call came for down tools for dinner, a plank in the loft broke beneath Harry's feet. He was left there dangling. Even worse, someone tied his feet together. And there poor Harry had to dangle while the others ate a hearty meal. And that was the last time he was ever seen around the neighbourhood.

And like Swift, the local old characters also disappeared, leaving us dangling in a uniform world.

13

Memories and Hopes

As a child among the old abbey ruins, climbing the walls and running around, one of the most sacred places in Wales was, to me, just a playground. The monks I had only seen in books, strange bald men in grey dresses and sandals. But as I grew older I began to realise that these strange people had been responsible for creating the character of the whole neighbourhood and had, in a way, helped form my own character as well.

Before the arrival of the monks in the twelfth century, no one had recognised the potential of the environment in the north Cardiganshire hills. Their contribution to agriculture, as well as to religion and culture, was immense. They were the first to realise that the value of the land was not measured in money but in production. They knew how best to develop the great potential. And, having produced stock and crops, they knew how to sell their produce and products.

There were sheep here before they came. But there was no plan. The sheep themselves were of poor quality, their fleeces of all possible colours. The monks bred uniformly white sheep and greatly improved the breeding. Having succeeded with the breeding they harnessed the rivers Teifi and Glasffrwd, forming dipping places and setting up woollen mills. They changed for ever the slopes of the Elenydd mountains.

They realised the potential of the meadow banks along the rivers and brooks, and planted orchards along the valley. It is strange to think that the first task the Welsh Patagonian emigrants undertook was to plant apple trees along the banks of the river Camwy. Side by side with the fruit trees, the monks developed vegetables and herbs for their own use and then sold the surplus at their various fairs.

Today, seeing farmers' markets set up in various towns is a welcomed sight. The monks set up such markets centuries ago, with their five annual fairs at Ffair Rhos. Despite the success of our farmers' markets, huge lorries still deliver all kinds of foodstuff from Europe. Have we lost the vision of the old monks who grew food locally to be sold locally?

What they did with wool, fruit and vegetables they also did with grain. They sowed oats, barley and wheat and built grain mills for the good of both man and beast. Today the majority of farmers are quite happy to depend only on grassland.

Not only did the monks depend on the arable land, they took to draining heaths, thus gaining more land for development. Today, hundreds of acres of the land they regained lie under the trees of the Forestry Commission.

Dotted among the hills behind the abbey are healing wells discovered by the monks. Many remain. More have disappeared. Farms in the area still retain the original names connected with the abbey. There is Old Abbey itself, site of the original monastery. There is Dolebolion (Foals' Meadow), Bryn Hope (Hob or Pig Hill), Dôl yr Ychain (Oxens' Meadow),

Llidiart y Ffair (Fair's Gate), Dôl Beudyau (Meadow of the Byres) and Mynachdy (Monks' House).

The monks were also fishermen, not only along the riverbanks and lakes but also along the shores of Cardigan Bay. At Aberarth they had underwater traps built of stones that would leave fish high and dry in them when the tide ebbed. Up above the abbey, at a place called Dyffryn Tawel, they would redirect the river for some two hundred yards, leaving a few pools from which they could gather the fish.

Today I can appreciate the great heritage they left for generations to come, all the way down to us. We look back at the monks mainly in terms of religion, education and literature. But, without them, our whole way of rural life would also have been so different. Their vision, and their realisation and implementation of that vision shaped the land.

But to return to latter days. Suddenly, my connection with the Young Farmers' Clubs was rapidly coming to an end. My twenty-fifth birthday was approaching, signalling an end to my eligibility for competing. Imagining life without competing on stage or the Rally field was impossible. But, I was fortunate later in landing a job that meant keeping my connection with young farmers' intact. But more of that later.

As noted, the YFC to me, and to hundreds like me, was a further education college. That fateful night when I was approached on the bridge by John Jenkins had been the key that unlocked a door I never knew even existed. It was John who also directed me towards the local agricultural show committee on which I served as secretary for over ten years.

It had been a chore that I took up with ease but found it very difficult to give up. Again, this was a job that brought me into contact with people and where I learned to try and keep an even keel in sometimes stormy weather. The show itself was a great success and is still alive and well.

When I was involved, the schedule meant staging the show during the afternoon followed by a horse racing meeting. The day would end with a concert or a drama at the local hall or a pint or two at the Black or the Red.

The races, in particular, were popular. There would be trotting races and what we referred to as 'walk, trot and gallop' combining all three disciplines. Jockeys came with their horses from all over the county, among them Rhys Morgan, Llanddewibrefi; Jim Powell, Trisant; Jones Talsarn; Jones Bwlch-llan; Humphreys, Cwmcou, Blaenpennal; Jenkins Talsarn; Morgans Cilcennin; Seaton Penparcau – and Father, of course. But as the tractor became established on every farm, the number of cobs and ponies dwindled.

The meetings, however, remained with the coming of the trotters, many of them brought over from America. Many of these had been crossed with Welsh cobs and ponies generations earlier. Other owners and jockeys came into their own, including John Evans, Llanybydder; Vaughan of Llanidloes; Parkes Llanfyllin; John Lewis, Henfeddau; Williams Rhiwonnen; Evans Alltmaen; Thomas Maesybont; Collard of Rhayader and Thomas Gorsgoch.

Our local show offered, even back then, a first prize of £100 for the winning trotter, meaning that we attracted the very best to Dolfawr fields. The land was freely lent every year by the Herbert family. There was much muttering when we offered such a prize but on went the show, and it is still going, although without the racing. Gone also are the plays and concerts.

It was at the drama after the show one year that Mari and I began courting. We hadn't met since our schooldays. Mari had been away working in London and had just been appointed to a teaching post back in the area. Little did I realise then that it would lead to what has been a marriage that has lasted fifty years. At school we had hardly spoken to each other.

It was at school as well that my English teacher mocked me, saying that I would never be able to put two English words together on paper. Yet it was to me that many neighbours came for guidance with their correspondences as bureaucracy became rampant. Aunty Mat would always tell me,

'You're exactly like your grandfather with your thumb in everyone's broth. Mind you don't get burnt!'

Fortunately, the broth cauldron is still bubbling merrily. It was around this time when Cardiganshire County Council decided that we needed a new fresh supply of water. It meant connecting Teifi Pools to the existing system. The pipeline was to cross numerous farms and I, as chairman of the local branch of the National Farmers' Union, was caught in the middle. I was the one who had to apply for compensation for the various farmers. After a prolonged campaign both sides managed to reach an agreement.

Complicating the matter was the need in numerous places to blast solid rock in order to bury the pipeline. In charge of these excavations was a gang of Irish lads led by Bill Murphy from County Mayo. Bill, the self-proclaimed Rock King, had never even heard of Health and Safety! Bill was probably the reason why such a law was later implemented.

Bill and his men used dynamite as if it grew on trees. Many were the occasions when a lump of rock would smash through a nearby roof. Tommy the Postman swore that one day, as he passed Bronberllan, a shower of rocks flew over him. Most of the roofs of houses in Terrace Road, Pontrhydfendigaid, were holed, causing the residents to believe that the war had started all over again.

Bill, however, was a very pleasant man who could drink Teifi Pools dry if they were filled with Guinness. Yet, I never saw him drunk. He would spend most of his time moving and drinking between the Red Lion and the Black Lion. One evening, as he charged out of the Red, he collided with William Davies, the Methodist minister. He apologised profusely,

'Jayzus, Father, sorry. Oi never saw yer!'

'Mr Murphy,' said Davies, 'take your time. Remember that Rome wasn't built in a day!'

And back came the reply. 'True, Father. Very true. And do you know why?'

'No, I don't.'

'Because Bill Murphy wasn't the bloody contractor!'

And off he went, leaving behind a bemused Methodist minister.

Bill would usually depend on his own Irish navvies but would occasionally take on local labour. One such man was Tom Evans, known to all as 'Tom Two Year Old'. Somebody, years previously, had asked him how he felt and he answered,

'Just like a two year old.'

And the nickname stuck. Tom's job was to raise a fence each side of the pipeline as it advanced. One day, as Father passed, he noticed that Tom was stapling the pig fence upside down with the larger squares at the bottom. Father advised him to take the fence down and replace it the other way up to stop lambs escaping.

'What's the point?' asked Tom. 'If they can find their way out through the fence they can find their way back in.'

I was still working at home when we gradually exchanged our Shorthorns for Friesians. We bought a few female calves and a Friesian bull to join the existing herd. This resulted in blue-hued cows that were exceptional milkers. I remember one warm, sunny afternoon when we were haymaking that one of the cows was about to give birth. We brought her into the next field so we could keep an eye on her. But, somehow or other, she managed to escape into the nearby woods. Next morning she was back with the herd but there was no sign of the calf. I searched for days but without any luck. A week passed, and then I spotted it hiding in the undergrowth, too weak to stand but still alive. We called Evans the Vet and he couldn't believe that it could have survived there all on its own. And, as I tended it regularly, gradually it grew stronger and developed into a strong and healthy animal.

Around this time the Ministry launched its campaign to clear every herd of any traces of TB. We were fortunate enough to have one of the first herds in the area completely cleared. I felt quite proud going around telling all and sundry the good news. Then, one day, I was walking along the riverbank and who did I see but Lovell and his family of gypsies. We were allowed to refer to them as gypsies back then. And this time they had brought along with them not only the usual two or three horses but also a Jersey cow.

I went berserk and called Father and, after much debating, Lovell packed up and left. Lovell had five children, four of them girls. Three of the girls were married and they all travelled together as one family unit. The youngest was a tall, beautiful dark haired girl and I once happened upon her bathing naked in the river. That's when I first realised that there was more to life for a growing lad than riding a bike or even a horse.

It was through Lovell that I met up again with Tom Davies, our former village policeman. The summer of 1952 was exceedingly dry and Lovell and his family would fetch their water from the local reservoir, and they were suspected of bathing in the spring as well. Davies was informed and he laid down the law to the Lovells. They refused to move, so he called Father and I to help him move them on. The Lovells left, as did Davies shortly afterwards, leaving us to mourn the loss of a local bobby just as we had missed the road lengthsman.

I was working at home virtually for pocket money. So I continually looked for some other way of adding to my earnings. Therefore, I welcomed our neighbour Mrs Lloyd's offer to pay me for minding her cats while she would be away on her trips to London. She lived in one of the Pantyfedwen houses up above us. In fact, she had five cats, all Persians and all pedigree animals with posh names. I prepared a comfortable nook for them in the barn with straw bedding. For about a year everything went well. Then, one morning, I noticed that there were only four cats there. One was missing.

I immediately thought of John Jenkins. He would have an answer to my dilemma. And John came up with a brainwave. He had read of a cat sale somewhere down south. But 'south' to John meant Lampeter. The following Saturday I was on my way on Will Lloyd's bus to the sale at Victoria Hall. And one cat looked exactly like Mrs Lloyd's lost Persian. I waited impatiently for Lot 138 to be announced. I managed to buy it for £3.7s.6d. On top of that loss was the price of the fare. The new cat settled in well with her new friends and Mrs Lloyd duly came home and called to collect them. A week later she called and asked me,

'Did anything happen to my Lillyput while I was away?'

'No,' I lied, 'why do you ask?'

'She isn't as ready as she used to be to sit on my lap.'

Somehow I believe she knew more than she revealed, yet she continued paying me for minding her cats.

Little did I realise, around this time, that another old country custom was on the way out: that of driving animals along the roads on foot. It was usual for sheep and lambs on the lowlands to be driven up to the mountains for the summer and back down in the autumn. Sheep from Dolfor, some ten miles away at Crosswood, would spend the summer on our mountain and I would drive them there and back for wintering. The James family would show their appreciation by feeding me to the gills and giving me a sackful of apples from their orchard. On the way back I could, without the sheep, take a few shortcuts with the dogs, including crossing a suspension footbridge and then catch the Crosville bus. Between myself, the dogs and the apples, we would take up two seats.

Every autumn old Jones Waungrug, near Aberystwyth,

would come by bus to buy some of the older sheep. I would then have to walk them all the way to Waungrug, a distance of some twenty miles. I would leave at dawn with my three sheepdogs, Fan, Fly and Wag, and by the time the dogs turned the sheep onto Waungrug land it would be evening. Then it would be a slap-up supper with Jones, and out onto the road to catch the last bus home. But I would never leave without Jones slipping me a handsome tip for my trouble.

I kept Welsh sheepdogs back then, Wag in the lead and the sheep getting used to following him. Later I utterly failed in teaching a Collie to lead sheep. On the other hand, I failed to teach any of my Welsh sheepdogs to drive sheep in an orderly manner.

Before I reach the end of my first quarter of a century at the Abbey Farm, I must mention one event that could have ended up badly for me. Some of our hens tended to lay their eggs among the hay in the shed. Mam began to notice that they didn't produce as many eggs as usual. I went to investigate and discovered evidence that someone had been sleeping rough at the far end of the shed. I kept watch without alarming anyone.

Early one morning, I spotted the culprit sliding down the side of the shed. He looked hard, rough and furtive, and carried a sack on his back. He saw me watching and hurried off over the rickyard hedge and headed towards the woods. That was the last I saw of him.

I had long forgotten about the incident when some time later I saw in the *Western Mail* the face that had stared at me that morning looking at me again from the front page. Mid Wales police were searching for him following the shooting on Dyfi Bridge, Machynlleth, of Police Constable

Arthur Rowlands, blinding him. The man's name was Robert Boynton and be became known to the whole of Wales and beyond overnight. Fortunately, he was soon captured in Corris. Looking back, I still sometimes shudder when I think what could have been.

Despite all the work at the farm, I found time to visit Mari as often as possible at Ystrad Meurig where she lived. We duly got engaged and discussed the timing of the big day. The vicar suggested a Saturday in November. It happened to fall on the eleventh, Armistice Day. The vicar, Geraint Evans, announced appropriately,

'Let there be a permanent armistice in your home!'

And our armistice has lasted throughout the years. As we left the church following the service, John Jones of Pantyfedwen, true to the old tradition, fired a shotgun repeatedly, causing Aunty Mat to fall flat on her back, her face as white as a sheet. Yes, John Jones, yet another great character. His son Caradog became the very first Welshman to conquer Everest. The sadness of it all is that John didn't live to see that big day. How proud he would have been of his son, *yr hen grwt*.

But to return to the wedding. I had decided to continue working at home even though it was obvious that Father intended to carry on for some time to come. I could now give all my time to the sheep and cattle without having to bother my head with anything mechanical. I'm still totally ignorant as far as machines go. My only cure to a machine that won't start is to give it a good kick. But, with an animal, I will know immediately when anything ails it and also what ails it.

Despite all the harmony on the farm, I knew at the back of my mind that there would be no future for three families on the one farm. But it is always a tendency to leave things until tomorrow. And before I even realised it I was flat on my back in hospital in Aberystwyth. Whatever had affected me laid me low and I lost all my hair overnight. I was brought home but warned by Dr Davies not to do any work whatsoever.

Life during those weeks of enforced idleness was like being in prison, every day seemingly getting longer and longer. Reading the newspaper one morning, I spotted an advert relating to the post of County YFC Organiser for Montgomeryshire. I applied and, much to my surprise, I was called up for an interview in Newtown. Mari and I drove up over Pumlumon towards Llangurig, the car eating up the miles. In Newtown I entered the interview room like a lamb to the slaughter. It was only then that I realised that I was being interviewd by sixty people! And then another bombshell. The interview would be conducted in English!

As I left the interview room I felt just like Uncle Jack must have felt when he came home from the war: lost and bewildered. A few days later I was informed that I had been successful and would begin my new job in September. And so it came about. And, looking back on my first twenty-five years on God's earth, only one day can I think of that was worse than the day of the interview. And that was that first Monday morning when I entered my office in Newtown.

I felt bereft. I had left behind my dogs, my two ponies, my sheep and the farm. Only babies cry. That's what I had always believed. That morning I was a baby. And, there and then, I made myself a solemn promise: I would be back some day.

Little did I realise as I closed the door on my first twenty-five years that I was also closing the door on so many aspects of the life I had lived within a comparatively small neighbourhood. During that time I witnessed the end of horse power on our farm, the cart and the gambo gathering dust in their sheds. And the old narrow plough, known as the 'Llanfihangel plough', and the harrow and the grass cutter, the binder and all the other implements not taken away as scrap rusting among the nettles. I believe that our old shire horse Darby was the last survivor of its breed in the area. It was a sad day when Evans the Vet announced she would have to be put down. That day we felt we had lost a member of the family.

To someone like me who simply loved the mountain community, losing it left a scar that will never heal. I sometimes console myself thinking, had I stayed, it would have disappeared all the same. Practically overnight the words 'Forestry Commission' became an epitaph on the tombstone of the old way of life. One by one the farmsteads of the Glasffrwd and Tywi valleys disappeared beneath canopies of evergreen trees.

I remember Ned Garreglwyd and I returning from the mountain one November across the peatland of Tywi Fechan. Ned looked around and simply asked a rhetorical question,

'What kind of bloody trees do they expect to see growing on this cold heathland?'

But trees were planted and the trees took root. Within a short time the families of Nantyrhwch, Dolgoch, Nantstalwyn, Moel Prysgau, Tywi Fechan, Blaenglasffrwd, Hafod Newydd, Grofftau and Pantyfedwen were uprooted. Homes were lost, a whole community of mountain people that had a strength of character in their minds and embedded in their bones. They were carved from the very mountains that protected them. Every home had been built on the banks of rivers and streams, providing water for the necessities of life and work for the folk and their animals. Fish darted among the stones in the gurgling pools. Today, the lifeless rivers creep through pine forests, their water devoid of fish.

The mountain farmers disappeared, followed by their unique way of life, the exchange of labour, the sheep gathering, the shearing, the peat cutting, the harvesting of the sparse grass. Lost forever is the self-efficiency practised during even the worst of winter snow and frost. All lie buried beneath the regimental lines of green trees.

The small religious enclaves of Glanrafon and Cwm Moiro, where men, women and children knelt to pray and where they performed at small competitive concerts, are long gone. The Abbey School closed soon after I left. No longer do people set their watches to the whistle of the train from across the bog between Allt Ddu Halt and Strata Florida station. Beeching's axe severed that connection. Now only the north wind whistles. And Will Lloyd's red-and-white buses have long retired to their final terminus.

But let's look towards tomorrow. There is always another new generation on the horizon. A new generation that may bring with it a new beginning, new values, a new tomorrow.

We can but hope.

14

The Return of the Native

WHEN I LEFT the area at the beginning of the 1960s, there were already signs of the disintegration of the community, both social and linguistic. But compared to other rural communities, it was still thriving. There were three eisteddfods held annually. There was a drama party. The Young Farmers' Club and the *Aelwyd* – a branch of *Urdd Gobaith Cymru* / the Welsh League of Youth – were still thriving. The church and the two chapels still attracted dozens of worshippers.

When I decided to return to my native patch after almost fifty years an exile, I naively expected that the community I had left half a century earlier would have remained relatively unchanged. On my first morning back I walked briskly to the shop. There I was greeted by Kate Lloyd with the comforting welcoming words,

'Welcome back, Charles. I take it you've come back to die!'

No, there was no fatted calf for this prodigal son on his return. Kate, now in her nineties is, unfortunately, one of the few real characters remaining in the community. As for the shop, it is the only one remaining of the eight that existed when I left. I would soon realise that Kate's greeting summed up the true situation. This was not the place I had left. I had returned to a community that was in its death throes. I was now the stranger.

One of the first things I noticed was the disappearance of the two benches at each end of the village. Even worse was the fact that the local characters that used to congregate on and around them had long gone as well. Those rustic philosophers of my childhood and youth were interred at Strata Florida cemetery, just over the wall from where I had been born.

I had bought a house on the upper reaches of Lisburne Row, built on what had been one of Evan Hughes' fields. Evan was a patriarch-like figure, a deacon and precentor at Rhydfendigaid chapel. He was also the local butcher who kept the one shop that still remains open in the village. On my first evening back, as I strolled down to the Square, I passed houses of others long gone, such as Jane Davies and her husband, who was known as 'Dai Talaroo'. The reason for his nickname still remains a mystery. I passed John David Hopkins, the cobbler's, house. 'Jac Defi' lived with his sister Elen and later her husband Ted. Next door lived renowned poacher Ianto John. Then there was Hughie Jones' house. Hughie was both a postman and a taxi driver who always smiled.

I reached the Post Office on the Square at the end of the street. It was dark and desolate. The only reminder of the days of my youth was the iron hook in the adjoining wall where John Gwndwn Gwinau, shepherd and deacon, would tether his white mare while he visited the Post Office and the nearby cobbler's workshop across the street. The cobbler's shop was demolished long ago. All that remains to remind us older generation of the shoemaker's skills are the two cast iron lasts that decorate a window sill.

Those who had lived in the street when I had left were all gone. They had been replaced by total strangers. Doors that once remained open until late were now closed. I soon realised that Lisburne Row wasn't unique in its transformation. I encountered people that I had never seen before. It had happened throughout the village. Even sadder was the fact that the incomers were not young Welsh people. The great majority were from the English Midlands, many of them retired.

There were also families with children. Our local school should be praised for its effective teaching of Welsh. Every child in school is taught the language. But soon it will disappear as the natural spoken language of the street. The decline is already being reflected in the changes in names of local houses from Welsh to English. There was a time when I knew the name of every house in the village, as well as those who lived in them. But when delivery vans from Tesco and Asda arrive these days and the driver asks for the location of such and such a house, I find myself totally ignorant. I often feel that I am a stranger in my native parish.

On Sundays, our almost empty places of worship reflect the decline in religious belief. These chapels and churches used to be bastions of the Welsh language. To us children, God was a Welsh speaker. Local events connected with places of worship today are few and far between. We need to rethink the form and content of our services. We need to stoke the fire before it dies completely. As things stand, more and more places of worship will be sold off to become warehouses or abodes. Often, because of the extortionate rises in the cost of the upkeep of chapels and churches, selling them off is the only option.

The whole feeling of being Welsh is being sucked out of our communities. As well as the eight shops I mentioned earlier, we could boast two shoemakers' shops, two smithies, two garages that also sold fuel, half a dozen carpenters, and an equal number of stonemasons. We are left with one shop. Fortunately, the family running the business is Welsh speaking and their shop incorporates a Post Office counter. Fortunately again, both pubs are still open and thriving and are run by Welsh-speaking owners.

The three-day annual Pantyfedwen Eisteddfod is still held, although audiences have decreased significantly. The number of competitors remains high, with individuals, parties and choirs using the event as a stepping stone to the National Eisteddfod. Our annual eisteddfod, unfortunately, is one of the last remaining embers in a barely flickering fire. Yet, during the recent past, two highly successful national Welsh-language folk singing festivals have been held here.

All these changes are reflected in the surrounding countryside. Fortunately, the agricultural community remains Welsh in both nature and language. There are fewer units and, as a result, fewer young people involved. Many of those that are left leave for college and are then lost. Having graduated, there are no jobs for them here. They have no choice but to leave for the towns and cities, many of them outside Wales.

The once thriving Young Farmers' Club and *Aelwyd* have long ceased to be, and the clubhouse where we would meet is now a dwelling. Today, unfortunately, there are few leaders left. Were it not for the farming community, the Welsh language would be in even more dire straits.

When I travel the mile from the village to the abbey where I was born and raised, I greatly miss the various diversions I used to encounter along the road. I would invariably be stopped by a neighbour, roadman, postman or the occasional tramp. We would linger and chat and put the world in its place, both our own little world and the greater world beyond Pen-y-bannau. Today, people whizz past me in their cars or meet me as they walk the dog, merely nodding as they pass. If that, even. The postman, as he passes, waves from his red van on a round that Tommy the Post would walk. Despite the length of his round, Tommy always found time to talk and sip the occasional cup of tea in our kitchen. And there was George Edwards, the likeable roadman who would greet me, rest his long-handled shovel against the hedgebank and reach for his tobacco pouch and pipe. Thanks to roadmen like George, verges and hedges would be much neater than they are today. They had pride in their work. Often, a passing tramp would approach me, politely requesting a cigarette or a day's work, and often receiving both. Tramps back then were truly 'gentlemen of the road'. There are no tramps today, only beggars.

Today, as I wander up to Strata Florida, I dearly miss the old homestead. It was our family home for generations, and its own emptiness reflects a similar void in my own heart. Its door is now firmly locked and bolted. It's as if it has turned its back on me. Or is it the other way round, with me having betrayed it? The house and surrounding buildings now belong to a Trust that will, at least, ensure that they will remain and, hopefully, serve the local community as a centre of study and learning, turning back the clock to the abbey's original purpose. I now look forward to this new chapter in the Abbey Farm's ancient history.

Despite the feeling of emptiness and loss, something still lingers in these ancient acres of land that will forever remain a part of me. It runs in my blood. It is embedded in my bones. This feeling, although it sometimes keeps me awake at night, confirms that despite everything there is a path that leads onwards. It is, hopefully, a path that will lead to a new beginning for the whole community.

Hasten the day!

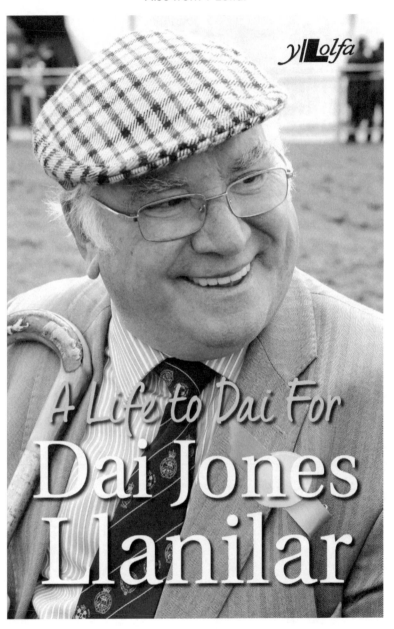

y Lolfa

A Life to Dai For

Dai Jones
Llanilar

£9.99

The Strata Florida Book Series

Charles Arch and Y Lolfa have agreed that this marvellous book about life at Mynachlog Fawr in Ceredigion will be the first in a series of publications about the history and lives of the people and their homes in this part of the Upper Teifi valley and Cambrian Mountains.

These will provide stories and background about the last few hundred years or so following the Dissolution of the Abbey, focusing on an upland farming community in one of the rural heartlands of Wales. We will call this the Strata Florida Book Series and develop a rolling programme of books which will be published by Y Lolfa in co-operation with the Strata Florida Trust which is conserving and developing the Mynachlog Fawr buildings for use as a centre for Welsh cultural heritage and history, telling the story of Wales at one of its most important and iconic monuments. More about this project can be found on www.strataflorida.org.uk

The series is currently in formation, but future ideas include accounts of the gentry families who once owned Mynachlog Fawr and the place of their estates in the life of the local people. We will also look at the farming way of life in the years immediately before the introduction of tractors, and how the new ways of supporting farmers began to change agriculture in the middle of the twentieth century. There is much to say too about the natural environment and the great beauties and rarities to be found in the landscapes of the region.

Ymddiriedolaeth
Ystrad Fflur

The
Strata Florida
Trust

Life Beneath The Arch is just one of a whole range of publications from Y Lolfa. For a full list of books currently in print, send now for your free copy of our new full-colour catalogue. Or simply surf into our website

www.ylolfa.com

for secure on-line ordering.

TALYBONT CEREDIGION CYMRU SY24 5HE
e-mail ylolfa@ylolfa.com
website www.ylolfa.com
phone (01970) 832 304
fax 832 782